Zodiac Manager

An Astrological

Exposé of

Everyone

in the Office

By

J.T. Ford

NEW PAGE BOOKS
A division of The Career Press, Inc.
Franklin Lakes, NJ

ZODIAC MANAGER
TYPESET BY EILEEN DOW MUNSON
Cover design by The Visual Group
Printed in the U.S.A. by Book-mart Press

To order this title, please call toll-free 1-800-CAREER-1 (NJ and Canada: 201-848-0310) to order using VISA or MasterCard, or for further information on books from Career Press.

The Career Press, Inc., 3 Tice Road, PO Box 687,
Franklin Lakes, NJ 07417
www.careerpress.com
www.newpagebooks.com

Library of Congress Cataloging-in-Publication Data

Ford, J.T. (Joe Taylor), 1940-
    Zodiac manager : an astrological expose of everyone in the office / by J.T. Ford.
      p. cm.
    ISBN 1-56414-560-3 (pbk.)
    1. Astrology. 2. Occupations—Miscellanea. 3. Vocational Guidance—Miscellanea. I. Title.

BF1729.O25 F67 2001
133.5'865—dc21

                                                                    2001031514

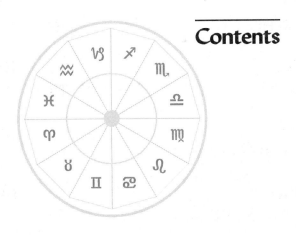

Contents

Introduction

As a creative director and writer in New York City, I was hired to design a motivational sales meeting for a prominent international high-tech company. The "show" was called "Reach for the Stars."

Because the theme celebrated the "stars in their business" I created a video award ceremony to introduce the company's top six salespeople based on their signs in the zodiac.

The idea was simply to introduce each top salesperson with a video of his or her sun sign announcing something such as: "With the typical persistence and commitment of a Taurus, star sales rep Fred Jones never gave up prospecting in a very tough and competitive market...."

Visually, it would be exciting, because the zodiac of the sun sign would be shown on massive video screens, then it would be transformed into a visual silhouette of the superstar salesperson. And as the winner came on stage, citing celebrities and movie stars born under the same sign would enhance recognition.

Couldn't go wrong, except for one troublesome detail: Four of the six winners shared the same sign. Four of the six top salespeople were born under one sign.

The first thing that occurred to me was, "Does their vice president of sales know this?" Clearly, if there are personality characteristics this one sign possesses that make for a winning salesperson, wouldn't management want to know this? And, further, if there are personality traits this sign possesses that make them less than productive accountants, wouldn't management want to know this, too?

In short, if different sun signs do, in fact, possess different abilities and strengths, both professional and personal, wouldn't that knowledge be valuable to the company?

Well, the answer, I discovered, is yes! Executives are using astrology as a business decision-making tool. And the number of executives using it is increasing as business demands more accurate personal information in its move to hire and retain fewer, but more productive, employees.

As author Michael Crichton confirms in his book *Travels*, "There is, in fact, a kind of secret level of activity in which psychics consult to major corporations and businesses. People seem embarrassed to admit this activity, but it takes place just as you'd expect it to."

In fact, it has throughout history. In the early 1900s, the brilliant financier and investment banker J.P. Morgan rarely made a move in the stock market without consulting astrologer Evangeline Adams, a granddaughter of John Quincy Adams.

More recently, investment manager Richard H. Jenrette wrote in his book *Jenrette: The Contrarian Manager* that he delves into his fascination with what makes people tick by using astrology as well as graphology and color-preference charts. In his book he even includes a table on the astrological signs of the leading CEOs of our day.

When *Business Week* asked Jill Barad, chairman of Mattel, Inc., how she describes herself she replied, "I am a Gemini. I am off the ground. I am definitely an air person. I am not calm. I am pretty stable but I am out there, thinking all different things."

"Chainsaw" Al Dunlap, when he was head of Sunbeam, had a ferocious feline hanging on his office wall behind him. When *Fortune* magazine asked him why he had a lion peering over his shoulder Dunlap replied, "Well, first of all, I'm a Leo. More importantly, the lion is a predator. And I love predators. They can't order room service, you know. If they want lamb to eat, they gotta go and slaughter it themselves."

Even a hardcore manufacturing-oriented magazine such as *Industry Week* got into the act in its March 16, 1998 issue. An entire article devoted to "Your Corporate Horoscope" trumpeted, "Forget education, experience and upbringing. The real key to your management abilities may be found in the stars." The article went on to give a capsule commentary on the characteristics of business executives according to their sun signs.

Fortune magazine asked astrologer/columnist Shelley Von Strunckel to interpret the Walt Disney merger with Capital Cities/ABC.

Even *Forbes* went on a recent star trek. The *Forbes 400* issue asked, "Which are the Lucky Stars?" The answer: Pisces are drawn to money like fish to water. There are more millionaires born under the fish sign than any other. Aquarians are second. Aries third. Poor old Geminis—literally. The twins come in last, with only 7 percent making the *Forbes* millionaire list.

"If *Forbes* is doing articles on astrology, then interest in the Zodiac has reached the highest levels of society," says Delos Greene, *Sports Traveler*'s sports astrologer.

In addition, Cathy Hainer in *USA Today* reports that the tie-in between business and astrology has company in other fields as well. Astrology has always been popular, but many believe this is just the beginning of the age of niche astrology.

From this book you will learn:

- What kind of a business dynamo you really are and how you can be even better.

- Who everyone else in the company really is and how you can make them work for you.

- Who your competition really is and how you can beat them at their own game.

These answers and more are in the stars! *Zodiac Manager* gives you the power to:

- Choose only dynamic high-performance employees.
- Identify only the most compatible colleagues.
- Pick the perfect secretary.
- Expose the innermost personalities of your competitors.
- Negotiate with vendors to get the results you want.
- Out-perform your internal rivals for the top spot.
- Know exactly how to attract a superstar.
- Choose the kind of team it takes to grow the business.
- Convince Mr. Big that the promotion and raise should go your way.

How to Use This Book

This book gives you the power to understand everyone around you by possessing only one single piece of information: the individual's birthday (or sun sign). And here are two ways to get it:

The Direct Method: Just ask. Few people are threatened by being asked "when's your birthday?" or "what's your sign?" In fact, discussing birthdays and sun signs is common talk around the office, and the office birthday party is an American tradition. But if you want to know without asking directly try the next method.

The Indirect Method: Subtlety. Without saying a word you can learn a lot from seeing flowers on someone's desk, several cards, or a box of candy. Or try conversation starters such as "Gosh, I'm just like a Leo," or "I don't think I'm anything like an Aquarius, do you?" saying, "Look what my horoscope says for today," or "What does your horoscope say for you" is another approach. Relating astrology to prominent people in the news or wearing a piece of jewelry advertising your sign is another way to jump start astral talk and reveal the information you need to use this book.

Of course, if you're the boss all you have to do is go directly to the personnel files.

Once you have the sun sign information, record the individual's name in his or her sun sign chapter. Then ask yourself, *What do I need to know?*

- **How smart is he?** Go to the "Intelligence Profile."

- **How loyal is she?** Check her "Loyalty Profile."

- **Does he have good work habits?** Go to his "Work Habits Profile."

- **Does she have eadership potential?** Check her "Leadership Profile?"

- **What job is he best suited for?** Check his "Job Skills Rating" or "Most Profitable Positions Chart."

- **Can I work well with her?** Check "Working Relationships" comparing your sign with hers.

- **How do I get him to do what I want him to do?** Refer to "*Zodiac Manager* Strategy."

By exposing who the people are who work for you, or against you, you will have the power to decide the following:

- Who can make money and who can simply spend it?

- Who can make decisions and who never gets off the fence?

- Who can get the job done on time and who always promises tomorrow?

- Who do you want in your corner in a crisis and who caves in at "Boo!"?

- Who do you want to chair a meeting and who don't you even need to invite?

- Who is the best candidate for supervisor and who is best in sales?

- Who can deliver that incredibly creative proposal and who is better off typing it?

- Who can you trust with the company cash and who should be denied petty cash?

- Who is after your job and who is helping you keep it?

- Who would literally die for you and who might turn state's evidence?

THE ASTRAL FAX: AN EXPLANATION

A dozen times within, we will interrupt this book to bring you an "Astral Fax" from the real world of international business. Please note that each "Astral Fax" doesn't refer exclusively to the chapter in which it appears, but to all of the sun signs. Look at each "Astral Fax" as a mini-consultancy. It is our response to specific business problems we've been asked to deal with. These "Astral Answers" to actual business concerns, questions, and challenges help managers use astrology to solve their real world problems.

I

Managing Aries

March 21–April 20
Symbol: The Ram
Ruling Planet: Mars
Element: Fire
Motto: "Me Myself and I"

A HISTORIC SAMPLING OF THE ARIES WORKFORCE

Jennifer Capriati	Howard Cosell
Isak Dinesen	Betty Ford
Aretha Franklin	Marvin Gaye
Emmylou Harris	Gordie Howe
Jane Goodall	Ali McGraw
Arthur Murray	Sandra Day O'Connor
Gregory Peck	Mary Pickford
Colin Powell	Pete Rose
Diana Ross	Rod Steiger
Gloria Steinem	Gloria Swanson
Arturo Toscanni	Sam Walton
Eudora Welty	Tennessee Williams

A Confidential Listing of Your
Aries
Managers, Employees, and Colleagues

Name	Birth Date	Position

INTRODUCING ARIES

This Fire sign, ruled by the warrior planet, Mars, is one of the most dynamic and enthusiastic leaders in the zodiac. Daring, adventurous, and competitive, this sign is constantly in motion. Challenges inspire Aries, and they are prepared to take a leadership role in overcoming all obstacles to success.

Symbolized by the assertive forceful Ram, Aries are confident that they are right. Expect frequent direct, argumentative confrontations with little room for compromise. Opinionated and secure in who they are and what they want, this sign does not suffer criticism gladly. Preferring action to meditation or contemplation, don't expect quiet moments or calm discourse.

With a great ability to communicate her ideas, this determined, take-action sign is a natural entrepreneur.

Aries Energy Profile

Be prepared for life in the fast lane! Aries talk fast, move fast, and think fast. This is an intense, high-voltage "action" individual, both physically (an athlete with energy to burn) and mentally (an active, creative mind in overdrive). When she's around, you know it. There's never a dull moment. Her presence is an electrical charge, "striking" everyone in the vicinity. You'll be drawn immediately to her enthusiastic and infectious nature. Then, slowly, you'll be won over by her charm and grace. Next, you will be vowing to follow her anywhere—or drop back and watch in admiration as she tackles challenge after challenge.

As Aries is always on the go, she likewise despises laziness or half-hearted efforts in others. Day or night there is no time for rest when Aries has committed to achieving a goal or overcoming an obstacle.

She's animated, restless, adventurous, and courageous. Expect an active traveler, passionately committed to going all the way and going there *now*. When you enter her world, you are entering a frenetic, urgent, high-speed, spontaneous environment; but then the mature Aries can also be the most unforgettable character you've ever met as she takes center stage and treats her audience to life as a celebration of the possible.

Aries Personality Profile

Danger! Drive carefully! You've entered "The World According to Aries!" Once you get past her considerable charm and personal magnetism, once you get past her enthusiasm and dynamic, pleasure-loving personality, once you get past the attractive, easy-to-meet outer layer, you'll find a fearless, assertive individualist who bends to no one—who is no one's property.

Aries is the source, the initiator, and a born leader. After encountering the charismatic veneer of the Aries, it will become immediately apparent that you are dealing with a helplessly ego-driven, aggressive extrovert—a "peacock" with an unmistakable "me first" obsession who delights in attention. Her egocentricity can be so advanced that she can consider everyone else beneath her. But don't expect Aries to realize how she is treating others. In fact, it will come as a surprise to her if you were to express you were hurt by her actions.

Self-reliant, audacious, and confident, she not only has complete faith in herself, but she honestly believes she knows what is best for everyone else as well. She is so self-centered, in fact, that she may consider your property her own—although she's not so generous with her property.

As with every leading actor, she loves honest flattery and needs it desperately. Don't expect her, however, to flatter *you*—and don't compliment others when she's around or you will unleash her jealousy. As you would expect, to be blatantly critical of her work will only serve to destroy the relationship and her respect for you.

This is a direct individual with little subtlety (or tact) and little time for gamesmanship, an uncomplicated, one-dimensional individual without a past (seemingly) who is what she is. Initially she treats others as if they had the same personality—treating them as facades or objects—in other words, treating them as insensitively as she treats herself.

As a result of having thought so little about "self" there is an innocence and childlike quality to Aries—a surprising immaturity in one so apparently confident. In fact, Aries has been described as "a kindergartner behind the wheel of a Cadillac." So when angered, you can expect a hair-trigger childlike reflex of the "enfant terrible" variety—either a temperamental outburst that is malicious and destructive or a passive silence, breeding sarcasm and creating disrespect from a distance. Clearly this aggressive, self-willed, and determined personality quotient of the Aries can make or break her, depending on how she controls it.

Of course, the ability to self-destruct will always be there below the surface. But if she is the type of Aries who has mastered her anger and vanity (if she has found a way to close the door, relax, stay calm, and reflect on what is happening) without submerging her dynamic and progressive individualism, she is on her way to having a distinguished professional career.

Aries Intelligence Profile

With "think big" as her motto, Aries nevertheless frequently has an average formal education. However, with her powers of persuasion, she's convinced everyone she's qualified to do anything; and although she probably isn't qualified, she *can* do just about everything! Mentally active (with a restless passion), Aries is naturally studious and retains knowledge easily— all kinds of knowledge, but minus the details, which she frequently overlooks.

Her outstanding mental talent, however, is her ability to provide "instant insight" into any given situation. Unfortunately, these quick, on-demand perceptions can lead to a simple understanding of a problem. Aires is an erratic mind making snap decisions and forming instant opinions, which she will defend to the death. Aries is a fast-talking, fast-thinking "promoter" and "persuader"—and an impulsive decision-maker. Reflection and laborious homework are not high on her list. Her approach to a given problem is straightforward: She understands quickly (usually in black or white), and she is also positive that she is right (and she usually is). In any case, she will have the only answer to the problem, so you can throw away the suggestion box.

She's not interested in rumor, gossip, details, abstractions, and complex viewpoints. The ideas that emerge from her uncomplicated thought processes are frequently ingenious—new ideas built out of old ideas or new methods built out of old methods. She is not the inventor; she is the pioneer, and with her high energy level, she has a fund of fresh ideas to try out in many fields. In fact, for Aries, the measure of her success is tied to her ability to make these ideas work.

Her success is also tied to her ability to avoid making emotional judgments in "the heat of the moment" and to her ability to avoid intellectual overconfidence (because her judgment/decision was undoubtedly made very quickly). Nonetheless, "instant insights" are part and parcel of her Intelligence Quotient, and, in general, that lightning perception is a distinct strength.

Aries Communications Profile

Aires is truly a gifted orator and a sparkling communicator! A glib, persuasive, world-class spokesperson that any company would be proud to have "out front." Socially, she is a witty conversationalist with a raft of fascinating and diverse stories.

A big fat warning, however: She tends to be argumentative and frank. Verbally aggressive, *winning is everything*, and she will even fabricate facts and engage in the expedient lie to win. Fast-talking and straightforward as well, her directness and her temper can turn sensitive people away.

Aries Diplomacy Profile

A first-class charmer or a first-class bastard, it all depends on her attitude at the moment and which facade Aires needs to achieve her ends. If it is a simple social occasion with important people, quite likely she will assume the role of the magnificent host or delightful guest and play the entire evening on that note.

Should a controversy arise, however, defuse her quickly or prepare for a nasty little war. Because her aggressive ego can always get in the way, she's clearly a risk as a diplomat, but when she's "on," she's outstanding.

Aries Money Profile

Aires has a better-than-average earning capacity in virtually any field of business; and she makes it easily. However, she enjoys spending it as much as she enjoys making it—and spending it on the *best* that money can buy. Traveling first class and glamorous surroundings are high priority to this show-and-tell performer.

This generous spender is motivated to making money because it gives her the freedom she needs to live an independent life, although she will take honor and acclaim over money any day. In fact, it's not totally the money but how fascinating the job or how visible the project is that will attract Aries. Job title and status are more important than money, as are frequent promotions to "showy" positions. Money is fun, but praise and power and excitement are what motivate Aries.

Aries Loyalty Profile

Aires is extremely loyal to her work, and that loyalty is unlimited once she has committed herself. Also, the bigger the challenge, the greater the loyalty quotient because it becomes a test of Aries's power to achieve. But she can also change her mind on impulse and be off to a more exciting project, so don't take an Aries' loyalty for granted.

On the other hand, Aries expects and demands loyalty from others. She is loyal to her closest friends; but cross her once, and you may never be forgiven.

Aries Work Habits Profile

Let's get this straight: Aries is definitely not interested in or adept at the nine-to-five routine of a desk job. No way! What she needs and is perfectly suited for is an *action* job with an independent, leave-me-alone work schedule. And don't worry: This is a genuine, enterprising workaholic—you don't need to keep tabs on her. Pressures, deadlines, and hectic schedules don't phase this "doer" in the least. Thriving on competition, Aries is most productive when she's working on new ventures or new angles where her initiative is allowed to flourish.

Don't, however, expect attention to details from an Aries. She is involved 100 percent in the "Grand Concept" and the "Big Picture" only. Forget the grueling homework, tight schedules, and problem-solving sessions. Endless hours of meetings and conferences are not for her!

An Aries must never, ever feel she is a "cog" in the machinery or that she is anywhere near the bottom or middle of the corporate ladder. In fact, whatever position on the job that she holds, she must be made to feel that she is in charge—that the initiative is hers to take. Because Aries considers herself superior to everyone else on the payroll, she should be given an important sounding title, the freedom to report directly to an executive officer, strategic salary increases, frequent promotions, and, in general, be made to feel that she has a personal pipeline to the "person at the top." (That is if she isn't the person at the top herself, which is frequently the case.) You see, the problem with Aries is that she can't stand to be a subordinate. She's too vain and too competitive. She wants to be boss, and she'll let you know it from day one. If you want an Aries to work for you, above all, you must honor her independent, commanding spirit. For it's only by working independently within the corporate structure that Aries can make money for the company.

Obviously, she can be a maddening and demanding employee. But her perceptions and ideas are financially valuable, and corporate rewards are gained in giving Aries whatever she needs. Her talents are considerable, but the cost of acquiring them can be high.

Aries Leadership Profile

Aries is a natural "showboat" (not a true leader) and a pioneering, enterprising spirit who ignites the office into an arena of great energy and activity! She is an individual with a superiority complex who loves to attract waves of followers.

In fact, all of her life, she has wanted to be on "top of the heap," and she has always known she would get there.

Aries the performer has a magnetic personality, which exudes a great personal energy, drawing people to follow her and work for her; although she searches for creative input from those who gather around her, rarely expect credit for your contribution. She alone must be "center stage" and her name alone must be on everything. Never expect her to work *with* you; expect only to be called upon to work for her. Her decisions are made unilaterally—no discussion, no advice necessary—unless she considers you her equal or a brilliant mentor. Only then will her loyalty and devotion shine through.

Aries honestly believes she knows what's best—and that's all there is to it! Be prepared, however, for some irresponsible, instant decisions as a result (such as instant hirings and investments).

Need we say that unmotivated, mistake-prone and/or bored employees will not be tolerated in her office—even though she is absent much of the time. For the hardworking, loyal, and creative employee, however, expect quick promotions and generous salary increases—provided that the employee can take the initiative and is ready to work any hour of the day.

Beware of a significant flaw: Aries is highly susceptible to flattery, which can easily distort her judgment of an employee's worth.

Aries Success Potential Profile

Aries prefers *monumental projects*. In fact, the greater the challenge, the greater the thrill, for this courageous and adventuresome commander is driven to attain exceptional and difficult goals. Worldly success is everything to an Aries (business is number one—forget her private life), and she is capable of achieving success. (When she doesn't, her failures can be as monumental as her successes.) Driving herself to the limit, she feeds on power and superficial aspects of success. Her motivation is ego gratification, and she wants it immediately—in money or, preferably, in adoration.

Aries can be the best employee you ever had—or the most impossible. But if she's properly managed and understood, few people can beat her at putting over the biggest deal you can imagine!

If you can connect with her and get her to reduce her ego, Aries can lead and inspire.

The mature Aries, however, is best suited to be an entrepreneur. She prefers to be her own boss and possesses the freedom to let her dynamic personality move outward and upward without corporate restraint.

She knows her aggressive, self-willed, and determined personality and temperament can make her or break her; it is exciting and challenging to her to be in control of her own destiny.

No doubt about it, Aries's goal is to be a *professional success*, and she can be extraordinarily successful! How successful she is depends on whether or not Aries is in charge of her energies and her ego and whether or not she decides to lead or to simply "show off."

ZODIAC MANAGER'S ARIES STRATEGY

- Give this employee wide open space to roam, wide open projects to tackle, and a wide open job description so that nothing is forbidden.

- Give her all the latest and greatest techno-equipment this warrior needs to do the job on site, wherever that may be.

- Make it clear that although she is the project leader, she has one person at home office she must report to—and that person must be a Taurus.

- Hand-pick her direct reports carefully. The one above must have Aries's respect and loyalty; associates below must be true believers and followers.

- Assign Virgo to track the project and handle all the details.

- Avoid putting Aries up against others in the company who are powerfully competitive (Capricorn, Scorpio, Leo, Gemini) or next to those she could hurt (Pisces, Libra, Cancer).

- Frequently download Aries's progress and analyze her work with great precision to insure results are what they are said to be.

- Provide a support group for those who work with Aries, listen to their concerns and problems, and offer meaningful assistance (because Aries won't).

- Pay Aries enough for her to live the glamorous life and "perk" the lifestyle with proper societal connections and the proper clubs.

- Give Aries a stunning office, highly visible, with "mucho" wall space for awards, plaques, and pictures. And drape an impressive title across the door.

- Make certain Aries has a prime spot at any corporate meeting or affair and herald her achievements whenever your public relations department can.

- For those moments when Aries has the wind knocked out of her sails or simply needs a retreat after a well-earned victory, give her a "safe house," a place where she and her superiors/associates can kick back, relax, regroup, and communicate openly and honestly.

Aries Most Profitable Positions		
Actor	Dancer	New Product
Advertising Executive	Entertainer	Development
Airline Pilot	Entrepreneur	Police Officer
Architect	Explorer	Producer/Director
Athlete	Fireman	Public Relations
Chief Executive	Head Hunter	Salesperson
Officer	Management	Singer
Consultant	Marketing Employee	Soldier
Construction Worker	Merchandising Executive	Sports Official
Creative Director	Musician	Transportation/Travel

Aries Most Profitable Location

Aries will demand an impressive, flashy, high-tech, and theatrical office in one of the world's glamour cities. She will expect big money to be spent for the highest quality furnishings of almost sinful comfort. She will expect an awe-inspiring title on the door and photographs of herself with the Board of directors, as well as the president of the United States, prominently displayed on her giant-sized, tailor-made desk. Everything in the room must reinforce "I am powerful": the highest priced coffee table books, designer desk accessories, a top-of-the-line computer; however, don't expect her to be in this elegant room very much. Aries's skyscraper office, high above the vibrant city, is only a stopping-off showcase. Her real work is done in a network of equally expensive hotels/restaurants/apartments/offices around the country and world.

Aries Job Skills Rating			
1 (Poor) to 5 (Excellent)			
Communications	5	Interpersonal Skills, Teamwork	4
Learning and Thinking Skills	1	Punctuality, Efficiency	2
Work Attitude	4	Loyalty	3
Creativity	4	Technology Skills	3
Problem-Solving	4	Self-Confidence	5
Decision-Making	4	Enthusiasm, Motivation	5
Money Management	2	Self-Management, Initiative	5
Flexibility	5	Honesty, Integrity	4
Accountability, Responsibility	3	Visionary	5
Planning Skills	2	Leadership	5
Details	1		

MANAGING ARIES'S WORKING RELATIONSHIPS

In General

You are bound to notice that the Aries's charisma attracts crowds, and she has many fawning acquaintances (she takes great pride in being admired by large numbers). But Aries needs very few close friends. So do not expect her to be interested in in-depth relationships.

Keep in mind that Aries is too impatient (which leads to misunderstandings) and too self-centered to work side-by-side with most people. Her need to dominate frequently precludes her effectiveness as a team player.

You will also frequently witness Aries's emotional immaturity, which can generate grudges and jealousies—and that same emotional immaturity allows a flatterer to be called friend.

Summary

Aries Working Relationships		
PROFITABLE	RISKY	NON-PROFITABLE
Taurus	Aries	Gemini
Virgo	Cancer	Libra
	Leo	Scorpio
		Sagittarius
		Capricorn
		Aquarius
		Pisces

Bottom Line

Aries with Aries

Expect great mutual respect and talent. The natural tendency here, obviously, is for each to dominate. If these two dynamos agree to cooperate, the results could be staggering—provided that detail-oriented people are hired to support this visionary pair.

Aries with Taurus

This is not an easy relationship, but it can be highly profitable. Both work in totally opposite ways. Aries will resent Taurus's plodding quality, but these two complement each other, and if egos can be deflated, the chance for financial success with this duo seems substantial. Neither will really understand the other, nor respect the way the other goes about her job, but each will understand and respect the profitable results. Still, expect some big fireworks along the way.

Aries with Gemini

Gemini is an unstructured Aries; and Aries is unstructured enough! There is very little compatibility here or profitable sharing of talent. These two creative big-picture individuals have nothing to gain by letting the other in on what they are doing. Jealousies are strong here, as is ego. This would be an iceberg vs. *Titanic* duo.

Aries with Cancer

In most cases, Aries will simply not have the time—nor will she care to make the effort—to put up with Cancer's complexities. However, Cancer can offer Aries valuable business smarts, and if Cancer can keep her emotional problems out of the office, Aries should be willing to pay well for Cancer's attention to detail. An Aries boss can use a Cancer employee. Aries is certainly not the humanitarian boss Cancer is looking for, but the more mature the Cancer, the better the chance she can make a profit for Aries. On the other hand, forget about Cancer as Aries's boss or both as co-workers.

Aries with Leo

Very similar personalities and a potentially exciting pair, this mutual admiration society could be dynamic! It could also result in some majestic business decisions. This is a big-league duo with big plans. The problem could be with their egos: There can be no boss. Only if each can agree to a 50/50 partnership will we see such spectacular commercial happenings.

Aries with Virgo

The Aries boss could certainly use a Virgo colleague to mind the office and dig into the detail work while she's out making the big deals! In general, this is an ideal business relationship because each brings vastly different skills into the market place. All that's needed is Virgo's respect for Aries' talents. If she can muster up those, these two are on their way to big profits.

Aries with Libra

The fast-paced, aggressive Aries has very little time for the less active, dream-oriented Libra. We find virtually nothing in common between these two. In fact, it would pose a potential disaster for Libra to try to run in the fast lane with Aries.

Aries with Scorpio

Stay away from pairing this duo! This is real head-to-head competition. Each is too egocentric and too power-hungry to work side by side. Both are out to be number one, and no compromise is likely.

Aries with Sagittarius

Given these two very strong, very independent personalities, it is difficult to imagine anything profitable coming out of such a pairing—simply because two such superiority complexes would be unable to yield or to share or work together on anything. Both are "stars" seeking the spotlight. Antagonism and competition result here, not cooperation. Given the intense energy level of each, they wouldn't have time to sit down and work anything out anyway.

Aries with Capricorn

Here we have two very dissimilar personalities, and it is difficult to imagine them working together for very long. The faster moving Aries has no time for Capricorn's more cautious style; and because each is a take-charge personality, they are bound to clash when it comes to making the decisions. Aries's unstructured, frantic, and commercial lifestyle, high spending and experimentation don't fit in at all with the financially conservative lifestyle of Capricorn who slowly grounds out results only after serious consideration. There's nothing to recommend the pairing of these two rivals!

Aries with Aquarius

These two will meet occasionally and share fascinating stories but soon each is off again, each on their very own personal adventure. If you can capture those occasional moments, you will be treated to some terrific ideas/stories/experiences, but don't expect that meeting to last very long. Both Aries and Aquarius know what they want, and both are strong enough to go after it on their own. They are much more valuable (and happier) working independently than as a team.

Aries with Pisces

Very little exists to recommend the commercial pairing of these two. The brash, energetic, creative, and self-confident Aries will find nothing special about Pisces and certainly won't take the time to discover her creative skills. Pisces, on the other hand, needs support and encouragement from her partner, and Aries is just not that kind of sun sign. Aries can easily hurt Pisces, and it's best that these two stay far apart from each other out in the harsh commercial world.

ASTRAL FAX # 1 :
MOST PRODUCTIVE WORKDAYS

When it comes time to hand out those big assignments, depending on the sun sign some days are better than others.

To get the most out of your employees, here is your daily guide to who's at their peak and who's not.

Aries:	Tuesday
Taurus:	Friday
Gemini:	Wednesday
Cancer:	Monday
Leo:	Monday–Friday, doesn't matter.
Virgo:	Wednesday and Friday
Libra:	Friday
Scorpio:	Tuesday
Sagittarius:	Thursday
Capricorn:	Monday–Friday, doesn't matter.
Aquarius:	Sunday through Sunday, all the same.
Pisces:	Monday, Tuesday, Thursday

II
Managing Taurus

April 21–May 20
Symbol: The Bull
Ruling Planet: Venus
Element: Earth
Motto: "The Rock of Gibraltar"

A HISTORIC SAMPLING OF THE TAURUS WORKFORCE

Andre Agassi	Johannes Brahms
Charlotte Brontë	Carol Burnett
Dale Earnhardt	Nora Ephron
Sigmund Freud	Ella Fitzgerald
Ulysses Grant	Audrey Hepburn
Ayatollah Khomeini	Olga Korbut
Sonny Liston	Golda Meir
Eva Peron	Anthony Quinn
William Shakespeare	Loretta Scott King
Benjamin Spock	Barbra Streisand
Johnny Unitas	Alice B. Toklais
Orson Welles	Tammy Wynette

A Confidential Listing of Your
Taurus
Managers, Employees, and Colleagues

Name	Birth Date	Position

INTRODUCING TAURUS

This salt of the earth sign is symbolized by the Bull and is one of the most practical, deliberate, and persistent signs in the zodiac. What Aries is to "action," Taurus is to "let's talk it over." Achieving the good things in life are of vital importance to Taurus, and the value of the dollar is revered.

Growth, development, and success are a top priority and when mature, expect Taurus to take over the top spot. This is when we see the power of the Bull emerge as he attempts to keep the status quo. Change is not part of the Taurean agenda, for it threatens the good life that it took him so long to achieve. Called the bankers of the zodiac, Taurean pragmatism will be valued by any business.

Taurus Energy Profile

Think of Ferdinand the Bull grazing lazily in the peaceful meadow. Nothing seems to disturb him as he goes about his daily business slowly, harmlessly, methodically, and predictably. He is comfortable and secure in his "verdant home" with everything he needs to make life grand—including his heifer. From all outward appearances here is a lazy, indolent, and satisfied creature living a fat and happy existence at one speed: low gear.

But we know this outward appearance is an illusion. (We know this Bull is in total silent control of his domain by his mere presence. We can sense the latent power concealed within this calm facade. We know he is the boss and the sultan of his castle.) We also know that if we were to invade the bull's turf, we would soon discover the full impact of that latent power. Threaten a bull and you can die by the horns; matadors face that challenge every time they enter the ring.

The power beneath this placid surface is immense; when unleashed it is hydrogen bomb time, scalding everything and anyone on its way. But leave the Bull alone and he is very happy, quietly controlling, in peaceful solitude, his kingdom.

Taurus Personality Profile

There are two personalities for every one Taurus. The outer personality we first encounter is as solid and enduring as the Rock of Gibraltar. Self-sufficient, salt of the earth, steady, and strong with broad shoulders—his strength and his unflappable demeanor in the midst of worldly chaos is to be received with awe. We feel protected in his presence.

His charm and warmth (and his wife's) immediately welcome us to his private protected world. We are his special guests and he will provide us with the very best in entertainment, as well as superior food and drink. And all of this sybaritic pleasure will take place in his showcase home draped in magnificent fabrics and textures, colors and tones, and under the loving care of his devoted wife. Fine works of art are found throughout and full-bodied classical music sends another sensuous diversion to the sophisticated affair. Other guests will include those you instantly recognize as "celebrities." And all the valuable and luxurious possessions, which Taurus proudly has on display, are also names you recognize as "pricey." It is as if you are on a stage set of a production of *The Great Gatsby* and the dialogue is correspondingly sparkling and ever so quick-witted (even if familiar).

In conversing with our Taurus host, he is quick to reinforce an observation that he loves to be surrounded by the sensuous, both in things and people. We also learn he is a staunch conservative and a devout believer in traditional values and principles. And his devotion to capitalism and hard work has paid off, giving him the rewards of life he has so painstakingly sought. At last he can claim the prize: the "good life." It was all he ever wanted. And now he can place his prize on pedestal for the entire world to see. This outer personality exudes the fear of failure.

From an early age Taurus is aware of his limitations. He is aware of the possibility that he may not, in fact, become financially independent, which is his goal. He is not as smart as his competition nor does he understand others' emotional makeup. He is aware of his superficial tendencies and the possibility that those wiser and more powerful than he will ridicule his ideas. Even when he has made it, he is aware of a materialistic beat and a "possessions are everything" mentality that tarnish his image. He is aware that he must protect himself with a game plan that is sharply critical of others, which can drive him deeper inside himself. And he is aware of the fact that far from being self-contained he must rely on a devoted woman and a warm and loving house to give him the security he needs to act out his public life.

Most Tauruses hide this inner turmoil very well. But when you see them strike out at others and become brutal and cruel, you know their defense mechanism has broken down and they've lost temporary control of their manufactured world.

It is because of Taurus's limitations that he feels he must literally design his own world—with cast, dialogue, sets, and props that support his plot—to achieve power through money.

Taurus Intelligence Profile

Taurus is aware of these intellectual limitations. It's as if he has learned all he needs to succeed and live well and that's it. Taurus is a self-made man and his self-made education reflects that. Learning from life's experience isn't really necessary, because he already knows all he needs to achieve his goals. Taurus is smart enough, it's as simple as that. And his frequent success often proves him right.

This lack of openness to others' opinions and the tendency to look at the world only in terms of black and white can create a stubborn, critical, and insensitive rather narrow individual who thinks only his way is the best way. This rigid attitude coupled with a superficial view of the events of life is nevertheless covered up rather well by Taurus's charm, savior-faire, and scripted monologues.

Curiously, Taurus considers himself a teacher. Particularly in one-on-one situations you will see Taurus teaching students the right way (translated "his way"). Not a lifelong learner, still Taurus learns enough to succeed.

Taurus Communications Profile

Socially, Taurus is glib, charming, friendly (in a forced sort of way), and even warm. He makes you feel at home very quickly as he entertains you with his well-thought-out remarks. Taurus takes his role as host very seriously and guests love his attention, flattery, and embrace.

In business, his chosen profession, Taurus is more direct and frank. He is a good and patient listener up to a point. Then he will want to know the results. He prefers efficient conversations free of detail or emotional sidebars. As detective Joe Friday used to say, "Just the facts ma'am. Just the facts." Because Taurus has very specific rules for business decisions, listen closely to what he's saying or asking for and don't get derailed. Communicate as he wants you to communicate and he'll come to you for answers.

Another way to make contact is to engage in an activity that Taurus loves (such as jogging) and gain his trust. Doors will open.

Taurus Diplomacy Profile

Taurus's performing nature in social situations makes him a striking choice as company diplomat. In these settings, he is civil, polite, ever so proper, and graciously charming. He knows how to entertain and win over others. He would never think of insulting or embarrassing. In fact, his tendency to prepare his remarks in advance holds him in good stead and prevents him from straying into unpopular subjects. With Taurus the first to greet guests at the door, they will enter smiling. In Taurus's game plan for success, diplomacy is one of the means to the end, so naturally he's a pro at it.

Taurus Money Profile

From day one, Taurus's favorite game was Monopoly. No sign in the heavens is as good at making money, investing money, and spending money than Taurus. This is "money man." It is the only sign that has as its goal to make money. True, his ultimate goal is power, but it is achieved by wealth.

A deep-seeded fear of financial dependence is what drives Taurus to accumulate wealth. With dependence he loses his freedom and his ability to control both the situation and those inhabiting it.

It is because of this fixation on money and the possessions and trappings it brings that Taurus gets the rap of being "superficial." Taurus's status- conscious "possessions are everything" motto does not leave room for serious intellectual development.

Although adept at investing and purchasing, Taurus is also a core giver and very generous to those who have won his trust, whether in need or not. Indeed, philanthropy is high on his list.

Taurus also uses his money to provide him with the kind of opulent retreat he needs for security. His showcase home is also his escape and his frequently sensuous possessions detract from the real world where he feels more vulnerable and insecure. For Taurus money does buy happiness.

Taurus Relationship Profile

Taurus has solid-gold relationships with his spouse and family. This is the key to his castle. The home means security and pleasure—the rewards of success—and the one who keeps it going strong will have Taurus's life-long devotion and love.

"Celebrity" guests and society's pretty people are acquaintances who add to the sensuousness of the Taurean lifestyle.

Taurus also forms relationships where there is mutual trust—trust generally won by doing the job right. These efficient, effective workers handle the details and complete the project begun by Taurus allowing him to take the day off. Close friends—few, if any. But not a problem for Taurus—his plate if full enough.

Taurus Loyalty Profile

Aside from loyalty to his spouse, Taurus is loyal to whatever or who-ever makes him money. Just as his lifelong goals are simple and straight-forward, so too are his loyalties—both things and fun people. But he is also loyal to God, country, and free enterprise, which makes his success pos-sible. He's patriotic, God-fearing, and devoted to home, hearth, and capitalism!

Taurus Work Habits Profile

A dedicated worker, Taurus was born for business. Life's resume glit-ters with highly valued qualities: dependable, honest, loyal, organized, prac-tical, and hardworking. The bigger the challenge, the better. The greater the chaos, the more important his rock-solid stability is. Taurus exhibits great business judgment, but the decision-making process that precedes it is slow and plodding. However, it is best to wait it out, because his careful persistence will pay off big time.

Ironically, Taurus is difficult to manage in that he does things his way, not necessarily the corporate way. Your advice, experience, and position do not mean much to Taurus. He has revised his job to fit his methodical nature—a nature that he knows provides positive results. Comfortable with his one way to do the job, he will be angered by criticism.

At whatever corporate level Taurus is working now, it is important to understand that his goal is the top, and top for Taurus is head of an em-pire. And more than not that is where he will be found. The Taurus's drive for money, power, and prestige out-distances most zodiac rivals, and slowly, persistently Taurus emerges number one.

Once number one, he makes the assumption that everyone in the com-pany is the same kind of self-made man that he is. He will expect people to do things his way and they will be rewarded on that basis. However, until you are able to work just as Taurus does, he will be patient. He won't ex-pect miracles and he will give you that second chance. But there will come the point when you are either doing things his way or you're out or pun-ished. Neither suggestions, criticisms, nor new ideas are particularly wel-comed because Taurus doesn't tolerate or need them. He knows how to succeed and all you must do is understand his "how" and do it. ("I did it my way and so will you.") In fact, Taurus counts on you learning how so that he can put the whole project he's initiated in your lap and let you do the day-to-day work so that he can return to the fruits of his success: his home, family, and possessions. After Taurus hands you the blueprints and the tools, he is off to enjoy the pleasures his hard work has afforded. It's as simple as that.

Although Taurus is creative and loves to dream big, he tends to subdue these romantic qualities in favor of an automatic escalator ride to the corner office. Only after he gets there does the romantic, sensuous, clever side show itself.

Taurus Leadership Profile

The boss is more like it; he doesn't see himself as a leader. In fact, he would be surprised and disbelieving if you told him that he led followers. He is a man driven by some internal thermostat to become important and wealthy. He has neither compassionate social cause nor issue to stand on. It's just that he wants it.

Other than his family's security and comfort, he doesn't have any agenda when he gets to the top.

Taurus Success Potential Profile

A born capitalist, the Taurus's drive must be immense (because so many Tauruses achieve their success). Torn by an inner and outer personality that could create a complex incapacitated personality, somehow the mature Taurus is able to uncomplicate himself and step by laborious steps to reach the top of the pyramid. Even when he gets there it is still not enough—there is still home and family to construct, for it is there he that finds his true reward.

Somehow Taurus is able to disparage the negatives in his "self," pump up the positives, and will his success. *Amazing creature—Taurus the Bull.*

ZODIAC MANAGER'S TAURUS STRATEGY

- Never underestimate the inner power of self-serving drive that Taurus possesses. Whatever his outer display—from calm to animated, from slow to entertaining, from quiet to charming—underneath there is ambitious raw power to be reckoned with. At anytime it can be unleashed. Be prepared for it.

- Because Taurus hides his true intentions so very well, astrology plays a much greater role in helping you understand him than it does with any other sign. However low on the company ladder Taurus might be at the moment, the insightful manager must begin immediately to release to the uneven personality. Early on you can begin to satisfy those inner needs the Taurus possesses: money, comfort, security, an undisturbed meadow, a social life, steady promotions, and applause for his hard work! In other words, give young Taurus the appearance of living the grand life he so desires and must obtain later in life. Your reward? Very profitable work from a true budding capitalist.

- Wherever Taurus is on the organizational chart he should be able to have some involvement with money. No sign in the zodiac can make as much money as the bull—so he might as well be making it for you. And because he is very organized, and responsible as well, your financial records should never run afoul of the IRS.

- Taurus will rarely come out and promote himself this way, but you should be aware of this irony: The practical, hardworking, earthy Taurus also has his head in the creative arts. As performer, mostly, but sometimes creator, the Taurus's magnetism is striking and dramatic, and he can mesmerize audiences. The accountant Taurus frequently moves aside for the performing Taurus and in the mature Bull he is superb in both roles.

- The enlightened manager will be very careful with who surrounds Taurus in the workplace—above and below as well as colleagues. Powerful signs such as Aries, Capricorn, and Gemini can cause dangerous fireworks. A Virgo certainly, or even an occasional Cancer and Pisces, will be more agreeable to carrying out Taurean marching orders. What you want to avoid is any volatile criticism of Taurus's work habits or any impatience with his slow decision-making process. Gemini, for example, and Aries—with their instant decisions—will simply try to overpower the methodical Taurus. And underestimating Taurus is the worst mistake you can make. Let me repeat, that for it's the most important thing to know about the Bull: *Underestimating the Taurus is the worst mistake you can make.*

- Taurus has few good and trusting colleagues/friends. To become one, always be honest and never flatter. Be willing to play student to his teacher; be able to mirror every business move he makes and shadow his values, beliefs, likes and dislikes. Get closer to him through a non-business-related activity (such as sports); be someone he can leave behind to do the work while he retires to the good life. You'll never really be seen as an equal but you will earn his trust and loyalty.

- "Get to the point!" Never over-explain to Taurus. He wants specific answers, not a lecture. He doesn't want "complicated"; he wants "simple." He doesn't want problems; he wants solutions. He wants short, efficient meetings, not two-day conferences. His business day will be filled with a series of minute-long meetings, and that is plenty of time to accomplish what needs to be accomplished. Think "true, false" exams, not term papers.

- In dealing with Taurus you will find yourself being less of yourself and more of him. But that is the only way you can get his attention. His "my way" of operating requires you to shed *your* zodiac and put on *his*. Results? He works more profitably for all and once he's out the door, you are your old self again. Call it "the Taurus Compromise."

- Beware the ultra-extreme: It's rare but it happens. Born in Taurus is the desire to build "empires." Some Taureans have taken that literally. When it happens, an autocrat/dictator personality emerges. This dangerous personality will do anything to succeed. Watch for signs of Taurean intolerance and cruelty. It is rare, but Hitler was born of this sign. And even on a lesser scale, there is a dark, insensitive, and potentially harmful person cradled within. Taurus tries to subdue this himself and frequently succeeds. However, there may be times when you may have to defend yourself or others against it. Defend carefully to avoid the notorious Taurus grudge—but defend, nevertheless.

Taurus Most Profitable Positions		
Accountant	Engineer	Psychiatrist
Actor	Entertainer	Radio Personality
Architect	Farmer	Real Estate Angent
Arts Critic/Appraiser	Financial Analyst	Restauranteur
Athlete	Forester	Singer
Businessman	Government Employee	Stockbroker
CEO	Interior Designer	Surgeon
Chief	Lawyer	Teacher
Construction Employee	Musician	
Diplomat	Photographer	

Taurus Most Profitable Location

To the workaholic Taurus, his office is his home. Above it all must reflect power and wealth, but in the best conservative taste. Whatever the level, Taurus will perform as if he is the CEO, and his work area must reinforce that attitude. The richly appointed office, with beautiful appointments and plenty of art, should also be isolated from the usual noise and traffic in the company. Taurus must have a quiet work area where he can work without interruption. And for maximum profit potential he should be working outside the city for a major conservative corporation.

Taurus Job Skills Rating			
1 (Poor) to 5 (Excellent)			
Communications	4	Interpersonal Skills, Teamwork	2
Learning and Thinking Skills	4	Punctuality, Efficiency	5
Work Attitude	5	Loyalty	5
Creativity	3	Technology Skills	4
Problem-Solving	5	Self-confidence	5
Decision-Making	5	Enthusiasm, Motivation	3
Money Management	5	Self-management, Initiative	5
Flexibility	2	Honesty, Integrity	4
Accountability, Responsibility	5	Visionary	3
Planning Skills	5	Leadership	5
Details	4		

MANAGING TAURUS'S WORKING RELATIONSHIPS

In General

Taurus's working relationships are more superficial than substantive. Because Taurus considers himself the self-contained, self-made man, he doesn't view others as essential to his success. When successful, he tends to be charming and generous to those around him whom he trusts and to the few he admires. He can also be frank and direct, even vicious, to those who don't meet his high standards. But aside from his wife and family, Taurus's relationships take back seat to the challenging but achievable goal he has set to reach the top. And *he* is really all he needs to achieve it.

Summary

Taurus Working Relationships		
PROFITABLE	RISKY	NON-PROFITABLE
Taurus	Aries	Leo
Cancer	Scorpio	Aquarius
Gemini	Sagittarius	
Libra	Capricorn	
Virgo	Pisces	

Bottom Line

Taurus with Taurus

There's too much ego here to work together—unless they are smart enough to see the profitability of their pairing. Stubbornness, jealousy, and possessiveness also become problems, and, of course, because both are after the top job, there could be constant conflict. Still, such a duo could be very successful and it's worth a try. Both respect the mighty dollar so there's an outside chance that opportunism will deflate egos long enough to get the job done.

Taurus with Gemini

A Gemini employee is made in heaven for the mature Taurus. This is the answer to his "creative" prayer. Gemini has all the brilliant innovation skills that Taurus needs to turn a sizable profit. And Gemini will find in

Taurus the understanding and the patience to work unstructured and on his own time. At some period however, Gemini will have to produce that commercially successful blockbuster. But Taurus is more than willing to want and provide the right conditions for success. Certainly Gemini will find Taurus slow and unoriginal, so they won't be friends, but the capitalistic Taurus cares about dollars over friends anyway.

Taurus with Cancer

Profit brings Taurus to hire Cancer. But in addition, Taurus has the patience and understanding Cancer needs to be comfortable, productive, and secure. They will never be friends, Taurus is too financially oriented for that, but Taurus's respect and support of Cancer should prove to generate a lot of money and a lot of first-rate ideas. In fact, Taurus is one of the few sun signs that produces bosses capable of dealing with Cancers.

Taurus with Leo

Both are often exactly the same thing: the top job with all the power and the wealth. If they were even wise enough to agree to work together this could be a financial blockbuster of a pair and a big league profit-making duo. But their personalities are so very different (slow plodding Taurus vs. perpetual motion Leo) and their egos are so strong and demanding that the result would be disastrously derisive. Each wants it his way and no compromise even seems likely.

Taurus with Virgo

Virgo is the perfect employee in Taurus's mind. These two work exactly alike: cautiously, thorough, paying attention to detail, and so forth. This is indeed a Taurean alter ego. Virgo will also have great respect for this boss and that's what he needs to operate best. This is another excellent profit-making twosome.

Taurus with Libra

The Taurus boss could use the creativity of a Libra employee. And the Taurus boss is patient and understanding of the less disciplined and less task-oriented Libra personality. On the other hand, Libra will find comfortable but assertive guidance from Taurus. But Libra will have to produce eventually or Taurus will call a quick end to it. Taurus requires profits at some point. If Libra, can deliver this is about the best commercial relationship he can find.

Taurus with Scorpio

There is an outside possibility that the financial wizardry side of Taurus will allow himself to work for or with Scorpio. And there is an excellent chance Scorpio will want Taurus to manage his financial empire. But these are two demanding egos, and sparks are bound to fly sooner or later. Nevertheless, if they can make it work, this is a mega-profit duo.

Taurus with Sagittarius

These two are total opposites: slow and conservative vs. motion and risk. On one hand, this gives the pair great balance, because they compliment each other's skills. But they are so different, they may be only able to suffer each other a short period of time. This could be a very profitable duo if Taurus is patient with the expensive, adventurous, and exploring Sagittarius. But he will expect Sagittarius to deliver big bucks in exchange for the freedom. It's a very chancy pairing but it's certainly worth trying.

Taurus with Capricorn

These are two very similar personalities: hardworking, conservative, committed, persistent, and purely capitalist. Slowly but steadily they force their way to the top. This is a powerful and successful duo, which unfortunately will find great difficulty in working together. Both Taurus and Capricorn want to be number one and to be in control. However, because there is big-league profit-making potential here, it is hoped that a partnership could be arranged with equal responsibilities on both sides. These are two very strong personalities and the balance would always be delicate; but the high-powered results are worth the risk. You'll know soon enough if it's going to work out.

Taurus with Aquarius

The moment the Aquarius employee walked into the Taurus's office, he would begin to feel trapped. Taurus knows only one way to work—by the strictest capitalist manifesto you can find. The freedom-oriented Aquarius would be totally shut down, his skills unable to operate in such a closed environment. Taurus could certainly use the brilliant, forward-looking, and inquiring Aquarius's mind, but because he adheres to his conservative rules, Taurus would soon restrict Aquarius from operating independently, which is the only way Aquarius can be productive.

Taurus with Pisces

The cautious, conservative Taurus boss has a great need for the futuristic, imaginative mind of the Pisces employee. And the Pisces employee will find Taurus to be a compassionate, caring, and patient boss. However, Taurus is a bedrock capitalist, and, if after all this careful nurturing of the creative, undisciplined Pisces, he doesn't produce, Pisces will be out and fast. The test is this: Can Pisces work under an eventual deadline and can he accept the fact that he must be commercially profitable for his commercial, yet sympathetic, boss?

Taurus with Aries

This is not an easy relationship, but it can be highly profitable. Both work in totally opposite ways. Aries will resent Taurus's plodding quality; but these two complement each other, and if egos can be deflated, the chance for financial success with this duo seems substantial. Neither will really understand the other, nor respect the way the other goes about his job, but each will understand and respect the profitable results. Still, expect some big fireworks along the way.

ASTRAL FAX #2: WINNING THE COMPETITIVE EDGE

Your competitor always seems to get the best of you. Who is that masked man anyway? And what kind of person can you put up against him to turn the tables?

How to Compete Against:

Aries: Outperform him with a big picture, Academy Award–winning Leo in tandem with the strong pragmatic intelligence of Taurus.

Taurus: Match Taurean street smarts with ambitiously practical Capricorn and add the persuasive, creative insights of Sagittarius.

Gemini: Use Aries to explore more inventive, opportunistic worlds combined with Virgo's ability to follow through and deliver.

Cancer: Sagittarius competes well creatively and forms even stronger more influential bonds to sell himself.

Leo: Aries's dynamic energy and futuristic insight combine with smart and earthy Taurus to cover more bases than Leo.

Virgo: The power and smarts of Taurus or Capricorn are more than a match for Virgo's power and smarts.

Libra: Decisiveness is key to competing with Libra, and Capricorn and Taurus are masters of the craft. Add Cancer's sensitivity to more human issues as icing on the cake.

Scorpio: It requires a combination of powerful signs to overcome Scorpio's intellectual strengths. Pairing the brain of Taurus and the excitement of Aries equalizes the match, and a dash of critical Aquarius should finish it off.

Sagittarius: Gemini is a good match for the energetic, exploring Sagittarius and gets the edge when you add the responsible Virgo to carry out the great ideas.

Capricorn: Taurus and Capricorn have virtually everything in common, but Taurus has just a little bit more of everything.

Aquarius: Virgo matches Aquarian smarts and adds the winning ability of doing the job on time.

Pisces: Cancer has the creativity to match Pisces, but it is the ability to be more businesslike and accountable that gives him the edge.

III

Managing Gemini

May 21–June 21
Symbol: The Twins
Ruling Planet: Mercury
Element: Air
Motto: "Let Us Entertain You!"

A HISTORIC SAMPLING OF THE GEMINI WORKFORCE:

Miles Davis	Bob Dylan
Clint Eastwood	Anne Frank
Judy Garland	Bob Hope
Rona Jaffre	John F. Kennedy
Henry Kissinger	Gladys Knight
Robert McNamara	Marilyn Monroe
Bill Moyers	Cole Porter
Joan Rivers	Dorothy Sayres
Brooke Shields	Nancy Sinatra
Harriet Beecher Stowe	Jessica Tandy
Marsha Washington	Walt Whitman
Frank Lloyd Wright	Brigham Young

A CONFIDENTIAL LISTING OF YOUR
GEMINI
MANAGERS, EMPLOYEES, AND COLLEAGUES

Name	Birth Date	Position

INTRODUCING GEMINI

The fact that Mercury rules this Air sign already says much about Gemini. In mythology, Mercury was the messenger of the gods and as such taught mankind to communicate and learn. Geminis are legendary as zodiac communicators possessing an unending thirst for knowledge. Interested in everything, this eternal student loves to share her discoveries with everyone. Bright and inventive, her creative and imaginative mind is fascinating to encounter.

Boredom is one condition Gemini must avoid. Her ability to learn too quickly (and superficially) and to speak too glibly are other dangers. Because Gemini's symbol is the twin, this sign is always doing too much at once. Concentration, persistence, and follow-through can suffer as a result. But this charming, witty, ingenious sign attracts many admirers whatever her weaknesses may be.

The business Gemini is most likely to succeed when the position and profession match her ingenuity and energy.

Gemini Energy Profile

You are about to experience a restless dazzling force with suitcase traveling in continuous motion, well over the human speed limit. It is a nervous, spontaneous, surging energy that accounts for this constant rushing about. There is always something a Gemini has to do, is on the way to do, has come from doing, and is late for whatever she is doing next.

It's in her blood. She must be busy, but never at one thing for very long. She must be incessantly occupied but also incessantly moving, physically and mentally, and always with more than two irons in the proverbial fire. Good luck trying to catch her; and if you do, good luck trying to keep her interest.

Impressive to watch and always the center of fun and excitement, this sign is more of an experience than a person.

Gemini Personality Profile

Gemini is openly charming with a dynamic personality that can take her anywhere, and wherever it takes her, she is the life of the party. Her charisma is contagious; her clever wit, glib conversation, and belly-busting humor are delightful. Thoroughly modern in her outlook and youthful in her appearance, this Peter Pan is always ready to take off on anything.

Frequently called the Court Jester of the zodiac, when this performer sees an audience she's immediately on stage with one of her many characters and with script and stage directions memorized, for she's performed these various roles many times before.

Gemini is Mrs. Popularity—your 24-hour entertainment channel. She's a great host and a great guest—count on her for *fun*. In social settings she is always the center of the action, which also earns her the Great Communicator Award.

The more you're with her, however, the more you see her mercurial side and her vast range of personality characteristics. For this is also a chameleon with several zodiac signs in one, who is one person yesterday and someone else today. Two people in one account for her unpredictability, and this explains why the constructive Gemini you met before may be a more destructive Gemini now. Tomorrow it will change again.

The multi-faceted personality not only accounts for her inconsistencies but also explains her occasional two-faced temperament. It also accounts for her interests in various fields and her attraction to many different people. This incredible adaptability can create a changeable and ambivalent Blithe Spirit that can be frivolous and capricious. To her, nothing is serious for very long. Life is a playground that she can look at or act in, but she does not have to actually live in it. (She plays at life more than lives it.) As a result, she frequently treats the world and people with a clinical, emotional superficiality as if she's playing with toys. A thinker, not a feeler, her lack of a sincere reliable emotional pattern makes her appear insensitive.

When she is not having a great time (which is what she really wants to be doing) she turns inward, struggling to sort out the mystery she poses to herself. (Who is the person underneath?) Although she spends a substantial amount of time examining herself, looking for the deeper meaning, she usually fails to come up with any satisfying insights. The reality is, she is a natural fantasizer with multiple personalities and it is difficult for her to distinguish between reality and illusion.

In her worst moments, she is superficial, a con artist, insincere, unreliable, impatient, and abrasive. And although she can be purposefully malicious, you can expect this, too, to pass just as the other characteristics of her personality change.

This unpredictable, highly changeable individualist is above all curious and seeks a wide variety of experiences. Easily bored, she is always moving on to discover "what's new?" Naturally, in the process she leaves things undone, but that never bothers this vibrant ego-directed powerhouse.

When Gemini is on, when she's exhibiting her great charm and wit, no one around looks better. She's alive, enterprising, and oh-so-clever. But beware her other personalities and get ready for the mercurial change.

Gemini Intelligence Profile

This is the clue to deciphering Gemini. At her best, this is a thinking machine, a creative idea-producer sending out solutions to a wide variety of problems. This is a genuine high IQ intellectual who thrives on mentally stimulating and challenging games. She's always learning, always asking "why?" Always investigating and always inquiring, she is a warehouse of information and ideas, and she uses them superbly.

Constantly searching for stimulation for her brain, she experiments with the new and the untried; and she reaches her conclusions so quickly that she regards herself much smarter than anyone else. ("I'm right! You're wrong!") Indeed, she is extremely critical of those who can't see the answers as quickly as she can.

The brilliant Gemini brain has several shortcomings. However, because this brain works so fast, it frequently understands and judges too quickly, rushing into decisions without using the full resources of her intellectually logical mind. These easy answers and snap judgments can create superficiality and a falsely earned know-it-all quality that does an injustice to Gemini's true capabilities. Although the brain generally works efficiently and effectively solving outside problems, it is inept at revealing the hidden deeper personality of the Gemini. Because of Gemini's wide range of interest, her brain may end up knowing only a little about a lot—and it may be too little to have much meaning.

The problem with Gemini intelligence is that she is so quick and so glib that with a little bit of knowledge she can bluff her way through absolutely anything. But whether she is a Gemini with the intellectual facade or the real thing, her mind requires constant stimulation in many different areas and it feeds off of this curiosity 24 hours a day. And when you listen to a Gemini talk you swear they know everything.

Gemini Communications Profile

Talk! Talk! Talk! This is an individual who can express herself with unbelievable skill on virtually any subject. This is the original Ms. Glib. This is Ms. Communicator. And this one of a kind, exceptionally superior conversationalist actually needs to communicate. In fact, the instinct is so strong that any profession not allowing this aspect to shine should be considered unprofitable.

Gemini can be a master promoter. Gemini can be a debater. Gemini can be master of ceremonies. Gemini can be an investigator. And she can do it all better than anyone else can. As someone once said, Gemini could talk her way out of hell.

On the occasional negative side, however, she can be carelessly flip. Sometimes she's no more than a gossip. And what you really want to avoid is her caustic, acidic tongue that can lacerate you with an evil wit, ridicule you, and overwhelm your opinion with reams of knowledge (fact or fiction).

But when Gemini is in top form no other sign masters the craft of communicating better than she does.

Gemini Diplomacy Profile

When she has her "charming personality" on, she can make everyone in the room have the time of their life. Glib, quick, and charming, she can solve any problem, avoid any embarrassment or disaster, and cover whatever uncomfortable moments may crop up. She can be the ideal peacemaker, host, and sought-after guest.

Gemini considers diplomacy a delightful game; the quests are pawns to be won over. Her broad knowledge and her quick, keen insight into what others enjoy hearing give her an unbeatable diplomatic edge. Naturally, we must always be aware of her changeable personality, but, in general, it's safe to say she enjoys the diplomacy game well enough not to get bored and switch gears.

Gemini Money Profile

She can be as erratic in her financial habits as she is changeable in her personality. This is an unpredictable spender who definitely needs a money manager. Because Gemini is an innovator she is willing to be a financial risk-taker and speculator. And she'll spread her money over a wide range of investments. Her willingness to pay for her fantasies and dreams can easily put her on the edge of bankruptcy. She is not particularly generous but will pay for revolutionary ideas that can yield a profit.

The more mature Gemini, however, realizes that money gives her the one thing she loves most: Freedom. Without cash she is dependent on the commands of other bosses. Without freedom and independence Gemini's "life as a game" is over. Because insecurity means slavery, the mature Gemini will store and invest her money wisely to guarantee she will always be her own boss.

Gemini Loyalty Profile

On the one hand—to herself, her ventures, fun, and the good life—dedication beyond that is either nonexistent or primitive. This is an opportunist seeking challenge and adventure.

On the other hand—those who overpower her with their wisdom, reputation, or accomplishments—can earn her loyalty.

Gemini Work Habits Profile

Gemini makes the office a delightful place to work with no dull moments. Her youthful enthusiasm and witty charm are infectious and, unless she is in one of her occasional destructive moods, you won't be bored around her. But you should be prepared to do a lot of her work for her—a lot of finishing up and a lot of straightening up. This is the original jack-of-all-trades with a wide range of talents and interests; she cannot stay at her desk long enough to complete a project or worry it through to the end. Easily bored, routine will immediately destroy her energy and her curiosity. But put her out front in a variety of exciting assignments and this charming showman will be unbeatable, impressing and selling the clients. Everyone will feel comfortable when Gemini's in charge of a social or promotional situation because she is a natural salesperson.

Gemini is a risk-taker and an experimenter with a raft of ingenious ideas to spread around. Many of them are worth pursuing, but you'll have to do it. You'll always find a string of half-finished jobs in Gemini's wake—while she's off chasing her newest fantasy.

Because of Gemini's multiple personalities, expect her to change her opinions and answers frequently. You can also expect Gemini to change jobs frequently or hold several jobs at once. Again it's the boredom and repetition that do her in. But you will want to try to keep Gemini's fertile, curious, and intellectual mind and her exceptional non-stop energy because of the profit this talent can generate. So you will need a most understanding and subtly manipulative boss to give her constant stimulation and to keep her headed in the most rewarding direction.

Above all, Gemini needs to feel free. She needs an unstructured, odd hour, unplanned environment that accommodates her spontaneous work habits. Regimen and discipline are not for her. It will take considerable effort to enforce even a modified capitalistic work ethic on this frantic investigator so that she becomes worth her keep, and that work must be directed in a way in which she feels no constraints. Job security is rarely the carrot that will keep Gemini. Admiration and support of her many endeavors and the salary to provide her with the good life are as close as you can come towards the assurance she'll show up next week.

You get the feeling that although she's employed by you, she's really working for herself. You've got to bend the rules if you want a Gemini employee. And you should have a Gemini employee for the range of creative ideas she brings to the company.

Here's a final caution: She'll think she's smarter than anyone else in the office is, including you.

Gemini Leadership Profile

Gemini is not equipped to be chief executive officer or president of any large association or corporation. She is too mercurial, unpredictable, and changeable to hold the top job. Her leadership could mean confusion and inconsistency.

If she is put in a position of great responsibility she must surround herself with expert administrators if the operation is to have any direction. Gemini could be effective heading a small creative group if she has a strong business manager she must report to on a regular basis (and if she is the head, expected to turn in immediate results).

But this basically non-leadership quality in Gemini can lead to an awkward problem because some Geminis will honestly believe they have what it takes to command. Because so many people do in fact admire them and enjoy the pleasure of their company, they will believe charisma is enough to run the show. But the fact is, it isn't enough, and unless they realize they need help, their sign could be disastrous. Conditional leadership with wise counsel is the only intelligent course for a Gemini leader. But in most cases, Gemini has no interest in a room at the top—or any place else, for that matter.

Gemini Success Potential Profile

Gemini is too schizophrenic to be a capitalist and to have that single-minded desire to efficiently accumulate power and wealth. She likes money and a lot of it, but she does things more for the excitement of it.

Gemini prefers an awesome challenge or a mentally stimulating game or a lively argument or a quest for a new solution. Constant adventure and stimulation is her idea of success. She is not ambitious or competitive in the corporate sense, nor does she have one strong cause she is willing to fight for. A laboratory full of games stimulates Gemini, not the daily grind of life. Gemini is a most valuable and innovative employee and should be courted by the capitalist, but she must be carefully managed if she is to keep her mental and physical energy active within the bureaucratic confines. If Gemini is free to inquire, her ideas alone can be a major profit center.

ZODIAC MANAGER'S GEMINI STRATEGY

- When dealing with Gemini in the business arena, be prepared to suppress your own desires and sit temporarily on the sidelines. Gemini is a one-person show—well scripted and well rehearsed. Interruptions only derail the performance. The time to work with or manage Gemini is after the show and before the next when she is toweling down and re-energizing her batteries. Her performance schedule is hectic and frantic but you must adapt to it in order to keep Gemini productive. Chances are by giving Gemini "her way" you will be amply rewarded.

- If you want gangbuster big ideas, listen to Gemini. You will have to sort through all the big talk very carefully, but as they say "there's bound to be priority in there someplace." Serious editing is required but the effort will be more than worth it. Gemini generates some of the best ideas of any sign in the zodiac.

- Be prepared to suspend corporate rules to maximize Geminis effectiveness and productivity. Her non-linear, rule-breaking way of working will be counter to most organizations, but you must trust that it's best to let her individualism operate at full capacity. Prevent others from observing this bending of the rules by isolating Gemini when she is preparing her performance.

- Create a "room full of toys" atmosphere for Gemini. This Peter Pan personality needs a playground in which she can explore new ideas and adventures. The more outrageous the setting, the more interesting her answers and solutions.

- Frequently showcase Gemini's gift of gab, brilliant wit, and powers of persuasion. Her role as spokesperson is a trump card you should play periodically. It will dazzle others and please your Gemini.

- Provide a supporting cast to pick up where Gemini leaves off. When she's finished with her show she will need detail-oriented others to bring the script to its natural conclusion. The supporting cast must fully understand their role and not complain but rather expect to come in and mop up.

- Identify the organization's legendary person of wisdom to serve as Gemini's mentor. Gemini needs a role model, too, and the only one she's seeking is the real guru. Gemini will learn from this exalted one and learning is vital, lest you get Gemini performing the same show over and over again.

- The bigger the challenger, the better Gemini performs. Don't be afraid to put her in charge when a crisis or an emergency arises. She'll take charge immediately and act.

- Be prepared for Gemini to have as many different answers and solutions as she does personalities. Decisions made yesterday may be made differently today. Make certain you update weekly what Gemini is thinking to stay in touch with her changeable mind. You will need to force the understanding issue, because she rarely sees her inconsistencies. Also, be prepared to "discuss" her instant decisions and judgements to make sure there is a solid intellectual or fact-based foundation to what she is saying. Don't let a glib comment suddenly become policy without looking deeper into the situation.

- Gemini is more insecure than she will let on. Be aware that inside she is still searching for who she is. She may reach the point where she needs help. Be prepared to provide professional "emotional" support to help her through this inner quest.

Gemini Most Profitable Positions		
Actor/Actress	Dancer	Merchandising
Advertising Account	Editor	Model
Executive	Entertainer	Navigator
Airline Pilot	Entrepreneur	Newspaper Reporter
Air Traffic Controller	Explorer	Physicist
Artistic Director	Historian	Promoter
Author	Interpreter	Public Relations
Cartoonist	Inventor	Radio/TV Personality
Chemist	Journalist	Researcher
Comedian	Librarian	Salesperson
Communicator	Life Scientist	Spokesperson
Consultant	Lobbyist	Teacher
Creative Idea Man	Management Consultant	Travel Agent
Critic	Marketing Manager	Trouble-Shooter

Gemini Most Profitable Location

Gemini is a traveler, a fast-paced adventurer forever exploring. Multitalented, she can do about anything and is interested in everything. Her office is the world, not a building with four walls and a desk. This is a curious intellectual who loves to share her excitement with others. Her life is an adventure no organized workspace could accommodate. Gemini's workspace is her brain, and whatever experience she is having at the moment is her office. All she needs to be profitable are herself and the freedom—away from desk and office—to pursue her latest interests.

Gemini Job Skills Rating			
1 (Poor) to 5 (Excellent)			
Communications	4	Interpersonal Skills, Teamwork	3
Learning and Thinking Skills	4	Punctuality, Efficiency	3
Work Attitude	3	Loyalty	3
Creativity	5	Technology Skills	3
Problem-Solving	3	Self-Confidence	4
Decision-Making	3	Enthusiasm, Motivation	4
Money Management	2	Self-Management, Initiative	4
Flexibility	5	Honesty, Integrity	3
Accountability, Responsibility	3	Visionary	5
Planning Skills	3	Leadership	4
Details	2		

MANAGING GEMINI WORKING RELATIONSHIPS

In General

She's fun to be with! This can be Ms. Popularity, the center of the crowd's attention.

Yet the fact is, as she treats life as a game, so she treats people: using them, exploring their ideas. In reality, people are toys and entertainment to her. They are the audience—her followers.

And although she can manipulate crowds or small groups, she cannot handle one-on-one relationships. Although she may appear to be a terrific partner or friend because of her popularity, in more intimate circumstances you'll find her impersonal or cold, even though a close stable relationship is what she needs most.

Gemini enjoys a few close-working relationships with highly stimulating individuals (as herself) with whom she can argue and explore. But in non-stimulating associations she expects people to look up to her and respect her for superior smarts.

Summary

Gemeni Working Relationships		
PROFITABLE	RISKY	NON-PROFITABLE
Taurus	**Gemini**	Cancer
Leo	**Aries**	Libra
Scorpio	**Virgo**	Aquarius
Capricorn	**Sagittarius**	Pisces

Bottom Line

Gemini with Gemini

These two will find great mutual stimulation in being together. However, how profitable they would be is doubtful. There is no efficient direction in this pairing to lead to solid results. However, if both are guided by enlightened management and charged with coming up with the great new ideas of the next decade, the end result could be awesome. Without guidance, however, expect only brilliant intellectual games.

Gemini with Cancer

Although Gemini could certainly use Cancer's office smarts, Cancer could be emotionally trampled by the elitist, coldly intelligent, manipulative Gemini. Cancer needs too much attention to work profitably, and this is a boss who could care less about giving it. On the other hand, Cancer could never boss the dynamic and overpowering Gemini nor could she work with her side by side.

Gemini with Leo

Try to make this work. It can spell big dollars with Leo directing Gemini. Leo will have trouble pinning down Gemini, but it can be done. There are a lot of similarities here and if Leo can get Gemini to be production-oriented, profitable results are on the horizon. The secret is for Leo to sell Gemini on the glamour side of the business and sweeten the Gemini pot with dollars. These two will also need a money manager to see that some of the profits are put back to work in the firm.

Gemini with Virgo

These two come from two entirely different worlds. Personalities are likely to be at war frequently. But commercially, Gemini would find great value in the variety of routine skills Virgo brings to the relationship. In fact, Virgo can bring a needed long-term stability to an erratic Gemini venture. But will Virgo respect Gemini long enough to stay? And will Gemini accept Virgo's demanding rules for a successful business?

Gemini with Libra

Libra wouldn't even get into the same race with Gemini. Nor would brilliant dynamic Gemini even appreciate the creative Libra dream world. These two will find nothing in common nor offer nothing to the other. They're two totally different personalities, with two totally different business attitudes.

Gemini with Scorpio

Scorpio is the ideal boss for the brilliant but erratic Gemini. Scorpio's single-minded drive for power will help her Gemini employee focus her talents in a most profitable direction. It won't be easy for Gemini to work under the dictatorial and demanding Scorpio, but there is big money to be made from this pairing if they can keep their emotions under control. There is big league productivity here.

Gemini with Sagittarius

This is a pairing of two of the most spontaneous individuals in the zodiac. The results of their efforts will be fascinating. Unfortunately, you may never see the combined results because they may choose not to work together (loners) or they may simply decide to go off in another direction. The most sophisticated management skills will be necessary here to produce profits. It can be done, but these brilliant unconventional characters are very difficult to guide together along the same path.

Gemini with Capricorn

Two very smart, coolly calculating sun signs here. They will get along very well on a mental level. However, it won't be easy keeping them together unless conservative, one-step-at-a-time Capricorn is willing to allow Gemini to continue to work in her fast-paced, future-oriented, and multidirectional world without restraint. There are big profits to be made here so it is certainly worth the effort to pair them. Capricorn needs Gemini's exploration and inquiry, and Gemini could use Capricorn's solid business skills to pull all the activities together into a profitable package. If each can be tolerant of their personal differences, impressive results will follow.

Gemini with Aquarius

These two have a great deal in common. They're two restless investigative minds with a whole world to explore. The experiences these two bring back are exciting. Their perceptions and insights can be brilliant. But work together? Why would they? Nothing really to be gained from it other than sharing fascinating wisdom. But these two are so independent and so detached from the commercial world that they can't sit around telling stories. They need to be off, alone, living them.

Gemini with Pisces

The self-assured, multidirectional, energetic Gemini is the kind of cool, calculating individual who can do damage to the emotionally fragile Pisces. There's nothing profitable about this duo. Pisces wouldn't be given a moment of Gemini's time and certainly none of the tender loving care that the creative Pisces needs to exist in the real world. The coolly intelligent Gemini has no interest in the daydreaming Pisces, commercially speaking.

Gemini with Aries

There's great mutual respect and talent here, but the natural tendency obviously, is for each to dominate. If these two dynamos agree to cooperate, the results could be staggering provided that detail-oriented people are hired to support this visionary pair.

Gemini with Taurus

A Gemini employee is made in heaven for the mature Taurus. This is the answer to her "creative" prayer. Gemini has all the brilliant innovation skills that Taurus needs to turn a sizable profit. And Gemini will find in

Taurus the understanding and the patience to work unstructured and on her own time. At some period however, Gemini will have to produce that commercially successful blockbuster. But Taurus is more than willing to want and provide the right conditions for success. Certainly Gemini will find Taurus slow and unoriginal so they won't be friends; the capitalistic Taurus cares about dollars over friends anyway.

Astral Fax #3: "Star" Number-Crunchers

Who do you put in charge of the money? Here's a quick rundown by sign:

Aries:	Speculation. Gambler. Victim of get rich quick schemes. Should seek financial advice not give it.
Taurus:	Prudent and cautious. Looks for safe reliable returns. Great respect for money. Controls expenses.
Gemini:	Spender. Risk-taker. Needs advisor.
Cancer:	Risky. Intuitive. Lucky. Goes with the gut.
Leo:	Flamboyant purchases. Quick to spend. Goes for show.
Virgo:	Cautious. Intelligent. Security important. Analytical investor. Goes for the long term.
Libra:	Not a strong money manager or investor. Must look to strong financial advisor to succeed
Scorpio:	Disinterested. Power more important than money.
Sagittarius:	Speculator. Gambler. Spender, not saver.
Capricorn:	Careful—safe. Blue chips. Sound financial approach to expenses and revenue growth.
Aquarius:	Wasteful. Unlucky. Makes poor financial choices.
Pisces:	Psychic. Goes with instinct. Suffers frequent financial setbacks.

IV

Managing Cancer

June 22–July 23
Symbol: The Crab
Ruling Planet: The Moon
Element: Water
Motto: "Home Is Where The Heart Is"

A HISTORIC SAMPLING OF THE CANCER WORKFORCE

P.T. Barnum	Ed Bradley
Pearl Buck	Princess Diana
Robert Dole	John Elway
Bob Fosse	Rosy Greer
Tom Hanks	Angelica Houston
Helen Keller	Anne Morrow Lindbergh
Harriett Nelson	H. Ross Perot
Richard Petty	Nancy Reagan
Della Reese	John D. Rockefeller
Wilma Rudolph	Carly Simon
George Steinbrenner	Meryl Streep
Steve Wozniak	Babe Zaharias

A Confidential Listing of Your Cancer
Managers, Employees, and Colleagues

Name	Birth Date	Position

INTRODUCING CANCER

This Water sign is ruled by the waxing and waning moon, which also controls the ebb and flow of the tides. Like the changing moon and all the changes it controls, Cancer mood swings are notorious. This emotional and sensitive sign is ruled by its feelings. However, with its symbol the Crab, it can hide its sensitivity and feelings from the world by a hard outer shell. As a result Cancers have complex personalities that range from mature to childlike.

Devoted and loving to friends and family, Cancer is also determined to achieve his goals. The past is important, home is important, and money and security are important. When any of these are out of balance, Cancer can be aggressive. Although highly emotional, Cancer is stronger than he appears, so never underestimate Cancer's potential to succeed. Cancer's creativity, sensitivity to others, and loyalty are vulnerable contributions he can make to any business.

Cancer Energy Profile

Unpredictable. Severe vacillations depending on Cancer's erratic mood. His variable energies in any given pursuit seem to be determined by the degree of self-respect and security he is feeling at the moment. It is reasonable to say, however, that he is generally slow with a capital S, unless he is caught up in the emotion of the enterprise/thought. And, occasionally, to fit in he will simply mimic the energy of the group.

There is another dimension to Cancer energy, and that involves intensity. Cancer covers a wide range from laserlike focus and intense obsession to out of body daydreaming. Whatever the energy level generated by Cancer, it is regulated by his own internal thermostat rather than by any outside source.

Cancer Personality Profile

This is one of the most complex signs in the zodiac. Difficult to understand because he possesses so many contrasting qualities and contradictions, Cancer, nevertheless, is constantly trying to solve the hidden mysteries of his psyche. The key to the mystery is understanding that Cancer is ruled by his fluctuating emotions, and, until he feels in some control of those emotions, he will close up and withdraw. Thus he can appear to be shy, moody, hypersensitive, distant, and cold when in fact he is only trying to protect himself from external hurts.

Likewise, when his emotions are under control, he appears warm, compassionate, generous, and fun-loving, even wacky. The more mature the Cancer, the more he understands and controls his emotions. The fewer his fears, the more socially aggressive he becomes. Which Cancer will show up from day to day is impossible to predict, and Cancer himself will spend most of his life trying to balance all the diverse elements of his complex emotional network to escape this kind of Jekyll-and-Hyde existence.

Cancer is forever working on his environment to create a safe protected place in which he can exist. He constantly battles with his emotions to carve out a loving, romantic, old-fashioned home life with family. He is driven to find his own defined and defended world.

Cancer is truly a unique and sometimes inaccessible character with a life orchestrated by his own sensitive and variable self-image. He can be a superb host with a wonderful sense of humor. He can be a tenacious highly organized perfectionist. He can be a romantic, profoundly sympathetic and deeply sentimental. He can be a cultured, reserved conservative with a deep respect for the past and the lessons we can learn from it. He can be a hermit with a private, self-contained lifestyle, guarding his inner feelings with a protective shell. He can be extraordinarily intuitive, anticipating public needs, desires, and his hunches border on mysticism, but he is totally insecure about his own future. He can give birth to great dreams and creative ideas. He can be absolutely devastated by criticism and so great is his vulnerability (he can take offense at anything) that he is a prime candidate for psychotherapy. He can be an old-fashioned patriot who loves his country and the perfect father who loves his family. (Cancers need to be needed.) He can hide behind excuses being too shy and too timid to test his abilities in public. He can be one of the great worriers of all time, tense, snappy, and rude. He can explode with anger one day and say nothing about it the next. Because Cancer can be any and all of the above, he is in constant need of great love, understanding, and support to stabilize his changeable and super-sensitive emotional makeup.

Cancer is not easy. For a while it may be impossible to crack the shell because his psychological defense system is in place covering his vulnerabilities as well as his talents. He can appear a passive bystander, in fact. But there are layers of surprises underneath and qualities of great worth, and, if you are willing to invest the time and effort, you can find great love, kindness, loyalty, commitment, and caring.

Cancer Intelligence Profile

Although Cancer has a highly valued intuition, he also has a strong academic side. Cancer is blessed with a photographic memory so virtually everything he has seen, heard, and experienced is stored in his self-made brain. In addition to absorbing what is around him, he also reflects on his observation as he files it away. His respect for the past adds even more material to feed Cancer's brain cells. This human library has yet another dimension: a highly developed imagination and creative spirit.

What an intellectual inventory—intuitive, intelligent, thoughtful, creative —all bundled in one individual. And more, he is also a visionary. Therefore expect Cancer to be predictably upset with any criticism of what he says and believes.

But wait—there's even more. The auto-intellectual side is blessed with amazingly accurate premonitions and mystical foresight. Further, always be prepared for Cancer's unusual and sometimes outrageous interpretation of the facts. This is a special and different mind, which can help you see things in totally refreshing and innovative ways. However, support and understanding are the keys: Cancer will not open up his interesting mind unless he feels confident and secure in your friendship. On the negative side, when he's feeling emotionally vulnerable he will either say nothing or accept the popular opinions of those around him.

Cancer Communications Profile

Sometimes Cancer is personable, chatty, and talkative, although revealing very little of himself. Sometimes Cancer won't say a word unless talked to. Sometimes he will script a conversation in advance to protect against his moodiness.

Sometimes, when he is expressing an opinion, he is a slow and careful speaker. Sometimes, he explodes with humorous and wacky observations. Cancer's conversational abilities depend on his mood and his comfort level with the subject and the people present. Sometimes, he is so worried about being contradicted it can be difficult to get him to say anything of substance, which is too bad, given his well-stocked brain. This deficiency and his genuine sympathy for others, however, combine to make him a wonderful listener. And remember: Cancer lockjaw can be overcome if you make him feel comfortable, respected, and a valuable contributor.

Cancer Diplomacy Profile

When he is at his prime he is a wonderful goodwill ambassador and friendly host. Not interested in promoting himself or speaking out on an issue, he is more than willing to provide for the good time of others. His facile social charm, courtesy, and natural tendency to listen come in very handy here of course. Cancer's diplomatic sheen is another example of his defense system protecting himself, but in this circumstance it has real value. When his self-image is in good shape he will love this game and be good at it. However, if disharmony enters the picture, he'll have trouble righting the occasion back to normal.

Cancer Money Profile

Cancer works hard for one thing: money. And there can never be too much of it, because money means security. And he is good at making money, investing money, and spending money. Money is not only a security blanket but it will also be used to tastefully decorate his home and lifestyle.

As compassionate as Cancer can be with good friends, because he is so passionately driven by dollars, Cancer will appear stingy and greedy to them—and with reason. Cancer believes that because all it takes is hard work to make money, there is no excuse why others can't make it as well. Cancer's vulnerability is at play here as well. He believes he will also need a stockpile in reserve in case his self-designed world starts falling apart.

Cancer Loyalty Profile

Cancer is forever loyal and loving to those who have never hurt him or let him down. Loyal to family and country, Cancer will never forget your friendship. It is extremely difficult to win Cancer's loyalty, but if you have been caring and made him feel totally secure, he's yours—although because of his many moods, you won't always know it. Cancer wants to be devoted and to receive devotion. He wants to be appreciated and feel welcome. As private as Cancer can appear there is nothing like the arrival of a good friend to put a large smile on his face.

Cancer Work Habits Profile

Cancer is half business, half emotion. On the business side (although it is very difficult to separate the two elements), you will find him working best and hardest in a large established business in an established profession (and as a group worker). His intention is to be a success and have an impressive career with your firm, and no other. Because he finds self-esteem through work, the mature business-minded Cancer is considered the perfect employee and his strong suits are indeed impressive.

His intuition and powers of observation are first rate. He can spot that new money-making trend miles away. He has a superb sense of timing and is an excellent organizer. He is a perfectionist. He is obedient, trustworthy, and devoted to his work. He is diligent, dependable, industrious, and will be proud to serve as manager in your absence. Cancer is a quiet, serious worker, thinking everything out and always finishing anything he starts. He is task-oriented and in a sense he takes his work very seriously and will lose himself in his work. Cancer is intent on doing the best job possible for his boss. Working in a calm, serious, office atmosphere, he won't fail to be productive.

Even in this close-to-perfect employee you still find several business shortcomings: An old-fashioned conservative, he shies away from change and frequently will be indecisive about things he isn't used to thinking about or working with. His shyness (and fear of being wrong) can prevent him from providing you with some of his usually excellent ideas. (He needs a little coaxing.) His lack of confidence can severely hamper his competitiveness, and because he is uncertain of himself he does not work well under pressure.

However, Cancer's positive business qualities are strong enough to make him an unbeatable employee, and if you want even more out of him, be sure to allow him space for his creativity and his imagination, which are, in fact, great strengths.

On the emotion side, he can be difficult. His moodiness and hard shell defensiveness can considerably diminish his contribution. Cancer requires an enlightened, humanitarian manager to use Cancer to his best advantage, to make Cancer feel needed and talented. Because Cancer takes everything so personally, pressure and critical supervision are definitely not the way to get him to do the job. Cancer is a very profitable employee only if conditions are comfortable for him and give him the feeling that he is valuable and appreciated. Cancer cannot work under just any kind of circumstances; rather, they must be tailor-made to support his sensitive emotional network.

Cancer Leadership Profile

The emotional, immature Cancer is totally unfit—this is, that Cancer whose anger and moodiness prohibits him from functioning in the market place. You can easily observe his sad, quiet, hermitlike demeanor.

And you'll find many other qualified Cancers who simply don't care about leadership or titles. Although they are very competent workers, they just don't have the competitive drive to take them up the corporate ladder.

However, there is a Cancer (the all-American Cancer) who has erased his emotional problems and taken control of his insecurities. Although they are few and far between, they are true leaders with great audience appeal (born executives or politicians). This Cancer is a professional—street smart, productive, a visionary, serious, hardworking, and fair. Employees enjoy working for him and he is most willing to protect those who are as dedicated as he is. (You will also be paid exactly what you're worth, if you ask for it.) While running an intelligent and profitable office, his experience has also made him teacher and you will have much to learn from him. This is an understanding boss who is not bossy.

The caution, however, is that few Cancers are even able to shed the emotional barriers that shade their lives and careers or even become competitive enough to fight for promotion. Insecurity inhabits many of this sun sign to the point that the very top spot is either unwanted or poses too great a risk to the company. Except for that rare career professional executive or politician, Cancers must be screened carefully before making any decision regarding the top spot—for their sake and yours.

Cancer Success Potential Profile

The more emotionally mature Cancer is, the greater his chance for success and profitability. At his best, he is excellent executive material with the patience and fortitude to accomplish goals long after others have given up. Unfortunately, Cancer can be his own worst enemy. This talented and considerate individual is frequently held back from success by his lack of confidence. The delicacy of his emotional nature frequently forces him into an uncommercial shell, and only the Cancer who can control his emotions can make the climb up the ladder of success.

It's strange, but Cancers have all the external makings of a success; in their healthy moments, they want to be a success—they want the money, which for them means security. But many Cancers lack self-esteem and retreat into a personal, intensively private world. Many Cancers choose the minor leagues rather than put up with the effort and struggle needed to play in the majors. Even when you find one in the big leagues, you always have the feeling he's still vulnerable to his emotions and fears.

ZODIAC MANAGER'S CANCER STRATEGY

- Once you have found a mature, highly developed Cancer, never let him go. This sign will bring with him the very best business skills: dedication, obsession with details, soundness with money, intelligence and creativity, serious work habits. Pay him well in money and respect. Promote him and reward him with the perks of life. Above all, become his true friend. If you do so, no better employee will ever be found anywhere. Plan well and you both profit mightily.

- Cancer will require and tax your patience. Complex and difficult, you are dealing with a puzzle. When the pieces are all put together you've got a great picture, but the struggle will be the time it will take to put them together. Each piece has an assigned place, just as each Cancer mood must be dealt with individually in order to create the big picture.

- Cancer can be his own boss. He knows how important his job is and he will never do anything less than his best to generate the results. He does need your support and admiration as well as your cheerleading, but there is no need to watch over him or monitor his efforts. To Cancer, work is sacred—a calling. It is his path to redemption and he will do nothing to demean it.

- Once Cancer is comfortably performing, avoid anything that disrupts this machinelike employee. He has worked hard to get everything under control. He is proof of his progress, and if his achievements don't derail him with sharp criticism or abrupt change, this robotlike employee has learned the best way to get things done. So don't do anything to break him or dismantle him.

- Make Cancer's workplace feel like him. Make it comfortable for him to "live" there. With his obsession for work he will, in fact, be living there much of the time. Set up a group around him of like character. Bring the concept of family to his position and his group.

- Make time to explore Cancer's imagination. You will be losing a large part of his productive capacity if you think all he does is the day-to-day detail work. Place no boundaries in your discussion. Cancer can go from developing a creative way to arrange the parking lot to creating a magnificent new vision for the company. This is an amazingly creative worker who can think very big and mysteriously. (He is said to have psychic powers.) In this case appearances can be very deceiving. Explore his world and watch him re-create yours.

- Given the massive internal battle most Cancers wage, make corporate life as comfortable for him as possible in and out of the office. This will prove better than therapy or medication. Respect and recognition erase a lot of Cancer genes and mood changes. The fact that "somebody likes me" goes a long way to creating balance and comfort.

- Find use for Cancer's teaching talents. All his observations, reflections, and readings should be made available to others. This is another way Cancer can build his own self-esteem while educating your work force.

- Provide Cancer with a thoughtful and understanding supervisor who can constantly monitor Cancer's emotional balancing act. At the first sign of unbalance, someone will need to move in to help right the listing ship.

Cancer Most Profitable Positions		
Actor	Dancer	Managemer
Advertising Account Executive	Dietician	Hotel/Restaurant Employee
Antique Dealer	Diplomat	Industrial Designer
Archeologist	Draftsman	Interior Designer/ Decorator
Art Dealer	Employment Counselor	Interpreter
Artist	Farmer	Inventor
Chef	Fashion Designer	Labor Relations Employee
Civil Servant	Film Director	Librarian
Clergyman	Financier	Marketing Manager
Clerk	Graphic Designer	Marketing Researcher
Commercial Artist	Historian	Merchandising Employee
Computer Programmer	Home Economist	Museum Curator
Construction Industry Employee	Horticulturist	Musician
Creative Director/Idea Person	Hospital Administrator	
	Hospital Staff Member	
	Hotel/Restaurant	

Cancer Most Profitable Positions (*continued*)		
Navigator	Physician	Retail Employee
Nurse	Plant Nursery Manager	Scholar
Occupational Therapist	Public Relations	School Guidance
Painter	Radio/TV Personality	Counselor
Parole Officer	Real Estate Broker	Secretary
Personnel Manager	Receptionist	Social Worker
Photographer	Research and	Teacher
Physical Therapist	Development	Veterinarian

Cancer Most Profitable Location

Cancer is a serious, creative employee, but he needs very special working conditions if he is to stay and remain profitable. One of Cancer's work needs is security; a well-paying job with a large, reliable, reputable company certainly fits the bill. Within that corporation, however, he needs a non-routine, freedom-generating position with a group of mutually supportive creative thinkers, as well as space for his serious detail-oriented tasks. Working in a calm, comfortable homelike environment with talented others and under an enlightened gentle supervisor, Cancer will produce big time. Cancer will perform even better if the company is located near water.

Cancer Job Skills Rating			
1 (Poor) to 5 (Excellent)			
Communications	3	Interpersonal Skills, Teamwork	4
Learning and Thinking Skills	3	Punctuality, Efficiency	5
Work Attitude	5	Loyalty	5
Creativity	5	Technology Skills	3
Problem-Solving	3	Self-Confidence	3
Decision-Making	3	Enthusiasm, Motivation	4
Money Management	3	Self-Management, Initiative	4
Flexibility	3	Honesty, Integrity	5
Accountability, Responsibility	5	Visionary	4
Planning Skills	4	Leadership	3
Details	4		

MANAGING CANCER WORKING RELATIONSHIPS

In General

Cancer has a remarkable heart—he is the original Good Samaritan. He'll do anything for his friends, and his concern and love can be unlimited. He also needs much love and care in return. Cancer's world can be full of joy or full of depression, depending on the people around him and how they respond to him. He needs support and appreciation from them. He truly enjoys people but, because they are unpredictable, Cancer's relationships can be fragile. His personal insights into the needs of others are very good, and he is a sympathetic listener. Still, his moods and his protective coating can put people off. Cancer, friendships require careful cultivation and an extensive understanding of his emotional complexities.

Summary

Cancer Working Relationships		
PROFITABLE	RISKY	NON-PROFITABLE
Taurus	**Aries**	Gemini
Libra	**Cancer**	Virgo
	Leo	Scorpio
	Capricorn	Sagittarius
	Pisces	Aquarius

Bottom Line

Cancer with Cancer

In most cases, this will be an unstable commercial relationship. This pair will certainly be sympathetic and understanding of each other's difficulties. However, there will be little agreement on how to get over the troubles and move ahead. Little of mutual value is seen here in terms of profit unless they are "kindly directed" by a patient leader. Alone, they can become stagnant. But it all depends on their individual emotional maturity. The greater the maturity, the greater the profitability.

Cancer with Leo

This can be a good match for both if Leo makes the effort to be a more understanding boss. Cancer will have a very difficult time working for the demanding high-pressured side of Leo and his world, but, because he can be profitable, it is worth Leo's time to protect Cancer and support his efforts in a low-key, more appreciative environment. Still this is a tricky pairing (both need to be needed) and how stable it can be is doubtful. But if Cancer is a producer, Leo will do what he can to make him very comfortable. (Cancer, of course, could never be Leo's boss.)

Cancer with Virgo

Cancer can no doubt use Virgo's superior business sense to make him commercially valuable. However, in the process, Cancer would become an emotional wreck trying to deal with all of Virgo's demanding rules for success. Only if Virgo decides that poor Cancer needs his loyalty and devotion in this cold cruel world could these two attempt a go at it. But chances are in the long run Virgo will run out of patience and respect and Cancer could be left comatose.

Cancer with Libra

Cancer and Libra can work very well together. Creatively talented, their personalities also mesh and they will understand each other's vulnerability very well. With proper commercial guidance the two should turn out profitable ideas. Don't expect electricity. And don't force them to move too fast. Just keep them on target and they should deliver.

Cancer with Scorpio

No question: Cancer profits from strong management, but this head of management would be lethal. Scorpio has no time for Cancer's pace and lack of competitiveness. Scorpio demands prompt productivity, and Cancer simply cannot work that efficiently. Obviously, Cancer should never attempt to manage Scorpio. He would lack the strength, nor would he find it worthwhile as a co-worker.

Cancer with Sagittarius

Sagittarius is the kind of romantic hero that Cancer can worship. But in the cold commercial world this relationship will produce little of value. Cautious Cancer simply cannot keep pace with the enthusiastic and adventurous Sagittarius. They're two creative personalities, yes, but they operate on different levels of the stratosphere. Except for appreciating his applause, Sagittarius won't even know Cancer is around.

Cancer with Capricorn

In many ways, these two signs are at odds. The more creative, aggressive Cancer will have difficulty understanding the serious, committed, capitalist Capricorn. Yet Capricorn needs a creative compliment to his personality, and Cancer is a good choice. Capricorn is usually mature enough to provide for the care and feeding of Cancer in such a way as to help him become more efficient and productive. Cancer needs help to become commercial and as long as what he offers can turn a profit, wise Capricorn management can help him realize that. You won't find a Cancer boss strong enough for Capricorn, but as long as Capricorn doesn't try to overpower Cancer or make harsh demands this could be a money duo.

Cancer with Aquarius

Aquarius is simply too powerful and too independent to hang around with the emotional and more cautious Cancer. In fact, the pairing would hurt Cancer. Aquarius grants philanthropic gifts or a helping hand to such people as Cancer, but he would never accept him as an equal. Cancer simply is not up to the world-class performing speed of the Aquarius, nor is he self assured enough to contribute to Aquarius's book of knowledge.

Cancer with Pisces

Pisces and Cancer will be shy at first and then attracted to one another. These are two compatible creative spirits who work on a sensitive and emotional wavelength. They will understand each other and support each other. Alone, they are not disciplined enough to be productive. If their creative ideas are to provide profit, a gentle, sympathetic manager is absolutely necessary to keep them on the commercial track. These two are capable of wonderful imaginative ideas, but whether they are moneymakers depends on a compassionate boss.

Cancer with Aries

In most cases, Aries will simply not have the time nor will he care to make the effort to put up with Cancer's complexities. However, Cancer can offer Aries valuable business smarts, and, if Cancer can keep his emotional problems out of the office, Aries should be willing to pay well for Cancer's attention to detail. An Aries boss can use a Cancer employee. Aries is certainly not the humanitarian boss Cancer is looking for, but the more mature the Cancer, the better the chance he can make a profit for Aries. On the other hand, forget about Cancer as Aries's boss or both as co-workers.

Cancer with Taurus

Profit brings Taurus to hire Cancer. But in addition, Taurus has the patience and understanding Cancer needs to be comfortable, productive, and secure. They will never be friends. Taurus is too financially oriented for that, but Taurus's respect for and support of Cancer should prove to generate a lot of money and a lot of first-rate ideas. In fact, Taurus is one of the few sun signs that produce bosses capable of dealing with Cancer.

Cancer with Gemini

Although Gemini could certainly use Cancer's office smarts, Cancer could be emotionally trampled by the elitist, coldly intelligent, manipulating Gemini. Cancer needs too much attention to work profitably, and this is a boss who could care less about giving it. On the other hand, Cancer could never boss the dynamic and overpowering Gemini, nor could he work with him side by side.

ASTRAL FAX #4: "STAR" SALESMEN

Who do you send out to sell? Here's a quick rundown by sign:

Aries: Great front man, but no follow through. Can win customers over big time but will need detail person to keep good on promises. Great at selling "showy" products and services.

Taurus: Use this sign to sell complex products and services that require authoritarian knowledge and expertise.

Gemini: Charming, intelligent, and enthusiastic. For big picture sales with glamour, this is the person. He won't be interested in selling the small stuff.

Cancer: Doesn't have the tough skin required for sales. Turndowns will be taken personality. Great at setting up meaningful relationships, but when things go sour Cancer walks away wounded.

Leo: Dynamic, fun, and a terrific showman people want to buy from. He needs backup to deliver the goods, but he can sell almost anything through the power of his personality.

Virgo: Honesty and a critical nature keep Virgo's sales personnel profile close to zero. Hype is not Virgo's game.

Libra: Indecision keeps Libra from buying into anything 100 percent. This is a personality customers like, but they will find it hard to deal with Libra's sometimes negative selling methods. The passion is lacking.

Scorpio: Comfortable relationships are not a strong suit. The powerful Scorpio frequently tries to force the products/services on the customer. Customers will eventually hide.

Sagittarius: The pleasing personality of Sagittarius and a natural sound nature make him a pro. Sagittarius must learn, however, that personality isn't everything. He will need to be made to become an authority on what he is selling.

Capricorn: Lacks that sales personality and interest in people. But he can be brought in as an expert to support the sales effort.

Aquarius: Isn't interested in selling, nor is there likely to be the total commitment required to believe in the effort. Persuading others isn't important.

Pisces: A frequently shy personality who prefers backstage. A frequently fragile personality that is stung by "no."

V

Managing Leo

July 24–August 23
Symbol: The Lion
Ruling Planet: The Sun
Element: Fire
Motto: Roar! (Translation: I'm the King of the Jungle and don't you forget it!)

A Historic Sampling of the Leo Workforce

Bella Abzug	Lucille Ball
Tony Bennett	Simon Bolivar
Emily Brontë	Roger Clemens
Bill Clinton	Elizabeth Dole
Jerry Falwell	Henry Ford
Mata Hari	Bernadine Healy
Ben Hogan	Whitney Houston
Mick Jagger	Jacqueline Kennedy Onassis
Stanley Kubrick	Herman Melville
Annie Oakley	Peter O'Toole
Beatrix Potter	Norman Schwarzkopf
Mae West	Esther Williams

A Confidential Listing of Your
Leo
Managers, Employees, and Colleagues

Name	Birth Date	Position

INTRODUCING LEO

A Fire sign, Leo is ruled by the brilliant sun (the source of all energy) and is symbolized by the Lion (King of the Jungle). Does that tell you all you need to know about Leo? However, behind the impressive front and the roar is a heart of gold. Leos love life, and they love being the source of that love and fun and joy life can hold.

Leo is also a stern leader, so don't be misled by the childlike pleasure she gets out of what she does. Confident, fearless, smart, and frequently manipulative, Leo is on her way to fame and success and she expects you to follow her or at least admire her as she marches on her way.

Leo is a natural business leader with the intelligence, strength, and know-how to manage others—as long as they don't mind playing second fiddle.

Leo Energy Profile

Whenever or wherever you meet her, she is on the go, leaving others behind! The energy of a perpetual traveler or athlete under pressure, she's ready to do anything and go anywhere, and she has the strength, stamina ,and endurance to match her continuous activity. An impulsive organizer, she will soon have everybody around her in her game, too, whether they want to be involved or not. Leo is full of enthusiasm and radiates a genuine desire to be noticed as she fills every minute of her life. Always in a hurry, (mentally and physically), most will find her frantic pace and nonstop schedule too demanding. However, after a victory, expect Leo to take a nice relaxing nap in the sun to recharge her batteries for the next challenge.

Leo Personality Profile

This could be the most memorable person you've ever met. Larger than life with radiant charm, she's the one who is always coming out on top! Leo is a Type-A super-achiever, the charming and impressive one, standing out in the crowd, the enthusiastic and dynamic performer, and the unassailable ego in the center ring craving attention and flattery. She is the daring, fearless woman on the flying trapeze, the boastful braggart out to win your applause, and the confident charismatic natural performer. She's the ambitious, natural show-off, the pompous strong-willed individual of excellent abilities, high goals, high ideals, and, yes, a bit of the domineering bully. She's critical of others and intolerant of criticism directed to herself, competitive yet resentful of competition. Of such stuff is the Leo facade made.

And yet behind this big front, Leo is affectionate, extremely generous, warm-hearted, and possessing great love—and needing it. She is a somewhat vulnerable lion whose roar is frequently worse than her bite, and a bit of a bluff. There is even an inferiority complex hidden inside and an insecure feeling that she could be better. In between challenges she can appear restless, bored, and even depressed. Never satisfied, Leo's down moments can seriously wound this Lion.

Leo has one goal: to rule. But her weakness is that she is prone to flattery, which can be used to control her instead. (Flatter her to get your way, ignore her and she's hurt and depressed.) Nonetheless she seems to recoup quickly enough to become king of the jungle once again and emerge as one of the most solid, dependable, and basically healthy individuals in the zodiac.

This is a single-dimension extrovert and center-stage performer who loves the spotlight. She is a performer in a play of her own making. She works and plays hard, and it's difficult to tell where one ends and the other begins. Her vanity and her bossiness can be quite unattractive, but Leo is usually sensitive enough to people to make up for any damage her "do it my way" attitude has triggered. With Leo, what you see is what you get, so you always know where she stands. But keep in mind that her image is created, as is her lifestyle. Her facade of power is manufactured, and she may never act out a personality much deeper than that.

Leo Intelligence Profile

Leo considers herself smarter than anyone else, and, no doubt about it, she is smart and a fast learner when she needs to be. Craving continuous stimulation, Leo is street smart and wise in the ways of the jungle. (Leo is also a know-it-all, even when she doesn't know it all.) This is a mind that prefers to deal with the big picture, which churns out majestic ideas. Leo is able to grasp facts and theories easily and is a solid constructive thinker. You'll never find her taking a short cut or learning superficially. This hard working mind also has an incredibly active and creative imagination. And when her mind is tested, she will simply claim ownership of the better idea and champion its cause as if it is her.

On the negative side, Leo is too intellectually vain to accept criticism or to be told she's wrong, and she is also highly opinionated. Unfortunately, once Leo learns something, she feels she knows it and that ends the discussion.

Leo Communications Profile

Leo is a forceful and articulate communicator—the star of the show, the lead player. She was made to be listened to: She's outspoken, direct, persuasive, and dominating in conversation. Leo will tell you exactly what's on her mind and exactly what she wants you to do. This is usually a one-way conversation (laced with humor), unless, of course, she is after an idea from you, in which case she is a very good listener. Leo doesn't have time to waste words so expect to have conversations of value on profit and not idle chitchat. However, behind the deafening roar, Leo is rarely as confident as she appears. But to hold the power in her hands, roar she must.

Leo Diplomacy Profile

The life of the party, Leo is a marvelous ambassador, a feat that she can accomplish by slightly submerging her arrogant ego. When she's on and performing, she is the perfect ringmaster in the theatrical arena. She is also smart enough to know when to direct the conversation on to other topics or other people. Impressive, entertaining, fun, attractive, and radiating a trustworthy strength, Leos are exceptional hosts, cleverly ruling and manipulating the event down to the every last detail.

Leo Money Profile

Easy come, easy go! Here is an authentic money-maker with a luxurious and extravagant lifestyle. Money equals power and importance to Leo, and she judges people by their wealth. A flashy dresser with expressive taste (she buys the best of everything), this is the last of the big-time spenders, a genuine high roller. Lording her wealth, she is generous to her friends and generous with her employees if they truly deserve it (if they've made her money). However, because Leo spends money whether she has it or not, she needs a first-rate money manager to budget her life.

A believer in "you've got to spend money to make money," Leo also expects to be lavished with money or other valuable perks by friends/employer/company.

Leo Loyalty Profile

Leo demands loyalty. She truly feels that she's so great she deserves unflinching devotion, and she will be deeply hurt and angered when she doesn't get it. (Admire her or else; be loyal to her or else!) Leo is loyal in return to those who genuinely helped make her a success. She is also loyal to her pursuit of success and power and to her ability to reach the top and rule brilliantly over her domain. However, don't expect Leo to be loyal to just one person. She is too social to be faithful to only one other.

Leo Work Habits Profile

The qualities that Leo brings to any job seem too good to be true, but she does seem to have it all. Look at this impressive list of Leo credentials. She's a genuine professional with a wide range of skills:

- Persistence.
- Creativity.
- Excellency under pressure.
- Expert planning and organizational skills.
- 100-percent productive.
- Punctuality and orderliness.
- Enthusiasm.
- Craves challenges (the bigger the better).
- Top-level decision-maker.
- Goal-oriented.
- A workaholic.

And as if that isn't enough, Leo is always "on." She loves holding court in the public spotlight, winning clients and colleagues alike with her persuasive charm. Leo is an impressive front woman who makes any company look very good.

Now here's the kicker: All of the skills just listed come with a steep price tag. You see, Leo wants, more than anything else, to be number one, the big boss. She feels she was born to command and does not enjoy having to climb the corporate ladder to get there. She wants to be the one telling everyone what to do and how to do it, and she doesn't take kindly to others telling her, regardless of their higher position in the company. Leo considers her superiors inferiors and feels that she is the one they should be looking up too.

If you want all this Leo talent, you must handle her with great care. Give her responsibility and control. Flatter her regularly. Tell her how much she's a credit to the company and let her feel superior. Put her in charge of training others. Avoid arousing her jealousy by playing up to others. Avoid angering her and don't promote the competition ahead of her. Give her the latitude to take risks (Leos are easily bored). Promote her and raise her salary with regularity. Show her off and let her perform. Give her a title and a very comfortable, dignified office or workspace. Give her an expense account to entertain clients.

Sounds as if you're doing too much for her and not enough for you? Well, we told you Leos were pricey. But the mature Leo is worth keeping and will give you a substantial and profitable return on your investment as she passes through on her way to the top spot.

It's true: Leos can be bossy, autocratic, and pushy. They love their freedom and don't like to be tied down in one place very long. They feel they are smarter and more deserving than anyone else in the place. They don't work along side anyone very well for very long. But they are so sharp, so successful, and so valuable that you don't dare be the one to force them out.

Leo Leadership Profile

This is where she has been headed in such a hurry all her life: the top! A fearless, charismatic, and dynamic leader, she knows this is where she belongs. And as the imperial ruler, she is accompanied by all the trappings and symbols of power and wealth. This is an impressive leader with superb organizational skills. From the presidential suite she directs her troops to carry out the details of the big picture she has painted for them. This is a demanding boss who expects you to be as good and as successful as she is, which is why she pays you well. This is a creative boss who nevertheless is not afraid of lifting your good innovative ideas and making them hiss. Boss Leo demands productivity or you will be out.

And, all the while, underneath this demanding tyrant, is a warm, affectionate individual who isn't really as cold-blooded as she appears. She absolutely needs to be revered and put on a pedestal by her work force, and the more you honor her and worship her the greater your reward and the more profitable her performance.

Leo is that kind of leader who wants everything done her way, and she sees to it that the company is a true extension of her desires. Leo is only happy when she's the boss. She needs to rule her kingdom. She needs prominence, power, and adoration. She was born for the life at the top.

Leo Success Potential Profile

Forbes magazine and Leo are both capitalists' tools. Leo gets the profits. Leo gets the sales. Leos have careers—rarely lives or hobbies. Leo's purpose and destiny are to achieve. Leo is the king and there is no limit to her material success. She's strongly motivated, certainly, but she is also inspired and possessed by the need to be at the top.

Beware however, of Leo depression, which comes from a neglect or inadequate appreciation. Leos are vulnerable, but it's rare that you see it sidetrack their drive to the imperial palace.

ZODIAC MANAGER'S LEO STRATEGY

- For all of Leo's power, she is possibly the most manageable sign in the zodiac. Why? Because you know her hot button: flattery. Careful how you do it and how much you do it, but do it when you need to get Leo to do what you want (not what she wants). Compliment her on the strengths she has that can make your project a roaring success. And cheerlead and advertise her efforts all along the way to the finish line.

- Make certain that the part of your business that Leo is in has a strong element of theater about it. Great performances are important to Leo, and you must be able to provide the stage and the audience for her to act. With smart manipulative management you can author the script and be the director, but your star must have the spotlight in order to give her Emmy Award–winning performance.

- The most difficult time you will face with Leo is when she is at the early stages of her career. She will want more than you can or should give her. She learns quickly and wants to move up quickly. This is when you can teach her valuable lessons. Let her think she knows more than she does. Then carefully (one on one) expose her to the subtleties and deeper dimensions of the situation—not to criticize but to give her the experience she needs to advance. Leo doesn't believe she needs to be a student. She's already the teacher, or so she thinks. It is dangerous for her to adopt this attitude so early in the game, and it's fatal for you. If she is ever going to learn it is on the lower rungs of the ladder, so don't miss this opportunity to teach her the ropes.

- Surround Leo with "gophers," with the people who are great at taking orders and doing the job—on time and on budget. Success or failure is often in the details, but Leo doesn't care about those. A strong support is needed to carry out Leo's directives and actually getting the job done in the trenches.

- When faced with your biggest challenges, call for Leo. To her, this is like being able to play Hamlet or King Lear. The bigger the part, the more brilliant the performance. Be advised that she will more than likely cover up with a brazenly creative solution that may shock and surprise you. But chances are, that's what is needed to overcome the major obstacles on your company's way to profitability.

- Be aware that much in Leo's life is fantasy, although she takes it as internally driven. Leo's internal concerns can border on defeatism and depression at their worst. When she has failed or has not been given a chance to succeed, fears of doubt arise. Pull Leo out of it immediately with another important role. Don't let her dwell on her emotions. She is not equipped to do so.

- It will not be easy for your top people to work with Leo, for she will absorb all the glory and the attention. You will need to motivate these people with rewards and perks of your own. Interestingly enough, however, although Leo does not have an empathetic working relationship with other top performers, she can do wonders when it comes to managing those with lesser skills. She has a generous spirit for those who need help and is a great teacher and inspirational leader for those lower down the corporate ladder. You stand to gain a great deal from this when you see Leo as trainer and coach of the second string.

- Leo's roar is worse than her bite. She can show her dissatisfaction in a loud, obnoxious, and even spoiled-brat way, but she can be calmed easily, and sensible talk soon emerges. Of course, when first experienced, the roar can be frightening, but don't let it turn you off. Work around it quickly and get down to business. Leo's moods can be easily and instantly changed so there is no need to let her roar disrupt doing business as usual.

- Leo benefits from a strong administrative assistant, someone to record all of Leo's directives, who is responsible for how much is being spent, controlling the calendar, and mastering details. Let Leo do what she does best: lead. Let the assistant keep track of all the rest.

Leo Most Profitable Positions		
Actor	Entertainer	Personnel Manager
Advertising Account	Entrepreneur	Politician
Executive	Explorer	Producer/Director
Airline Pilot	Fashion Designer	Public Relations
Architect	Head Hunter	Executive
Arts Management	Hotel/Motel/Restaurant	Radio/TV Personality
Employee	Manager	Real Estate Broker
Athlete	Interior Designer	Retail
Beautician	Lawyer	Salesperson
Chef	Lobbyist	Singer
Chief Executive	Manager (Planning)	Social Worker
Officer	Marketing Executive	Soldier
City Manager	Merchandising Employee	Sports Official
Commander	Model	Supervisor
Creative Director	New Product Developer	Teacher
Dancer	Office Business	Travel Industry
Diplomat	Manager	Employee
Editor		

Leo Most Profitable Location

It will be difficult to tell Leo's workspace from center stage at a Broadway show. She loves the glamour and the spotlights, and her office will reflect her highly theatrical flair. But don't expect to find her in it very often. Leo has many interests, and she spends most of her time out on the road exploring and discovering. Whatever and wherever her temporary workspace, it too will be on the spectacular side, but she won't be there long. Leo's offices are expensive and rarely used, but they are necessary showcases for her to show off her talents.

Leo Job Skills Rating			
1 (Poor) to 5 (Excellent)			
Communications	5	Interpersonal Skills, Teamwork	5
Learning and Thinking Skills	4	Punctuality, Efficiency	4
Work Attitude	5	Loyalty	4
Creativity	4	Technology Skills	3
Problem-Solving	4	Self-Confidence	5
Decision-Making	5	Enthusiasm, Motivation	5
Money Management	3	Self-Management, Initiative	5
Flexibility	4	Honesty, Integrity	4
Accountability, Responsibility	4	Visionary	5
Planning Skills	3	Leadership	5
Details	3		

MANAGING LEO WORKING RELATIONSHIPS

In General

With tremendous charm Leo manipulates her adoring crowd. But she, herself, is at a distance. Leo vastly prefers (and indeed seeks) audience worship to close friendships. Besides, on a personal basis her number-one attitude would be very difficult to deal with, despite her underlying warmth and generosity.

Leo does, however, collect the important, wealthy people—the elite. That makes her look ever more impressive and gives her the security of knowing she's important, too.

In general, people really like the social Leo because she's always on stage. Off-stage she's too bossy or too disinterested. You would think the delightful Leo would be more of a people person. However, because she is 100-percent driven to obtain leadership she only has time for people who can be of real value to her. Unfortunately, she also has time for flatterers and sycophants, as well.

Summary

Leo Working Relationships		
PROFITABLE	RISKY	NON-PROFITABLE
Gemini	Aries	Leo
Libra	Cancer	Taurus
Aquarius	Virgo	Scorpio
Pisces	Sagittarius	
	Capricorn	

Bottom Line

Leo with Leo

Although the value of having these two turning out ideas and directing the business is immense, it seems unlikely that we will ever see it. The egos and the jealousies would make such a pairing impossible. Two number ones, sharing the responsibilities? Forget it. These are competitors, not partners.

Leo with Virgo

Leo will have a solid, detail-oriented, perfectionist working for her. All those day-to-day problems Leo doesn't want to deal with, Virgo is pleased to tackle. But the easygoing Leo is going to have trouble with the overbearing and precise Virgo. And Virgo's going to have problems respecting a boss who relishes in showmanship antics. The duo needs constant monitoring and compromise to be as profitable as we know it can be. The money involved makes it worth the effort.

Leo with Libra

Although Libra's actual commercial value to Leo is suspect, boss Leo may decide her employee's charm to be just the ticket to promote her operation and to keep her clients very happy. These are two great frontwomen, and their good life personalities are wonderfully similar. There's no routine or detailed office work here, just the exciting big picture and the decidedly theatrical side of business.

Leo with Scorpio

Two competitors both looking for power, this pairing would be fiercely contested, leaving behind a great deal of destruction before it was all over. Each is after the number-one decision-making role and you don't need two of these types around the office. And don't expect Leo to work for Scorpio— or Scorpio for Leo.

Leo with Sagittarius

If you can get them to work together in an informal partnership, you should do it. These two are capable of brilliant results. But these independent showboating personalities won't be easy to keep on target. And what could be worse, Leo might try to take command. Big dollars are possible here in risky ventures. Stability and consistency are the problems.

Leo with Capricorn

Conservative Capricorn could certainly use the public relations and promotional skills of the dynamic Leo. This is an area the reserved, dignified Capricorn is weakest in. However, Capricorn doesn't respect Leo's flash. Capricorn is serious about her traditionalist reputation and her classy, tasteful style and demeanor. As far as she is concerned, Leo is a clown. But Leo is a smart clown, and her antics bring in business. Capricorn is aware of this, too, and as much as she doesn't want it, she will need Leo as a frontwoman. There will always be friction between the two, but they can be profitable together if they don't have to cross paths too many times.

Leo with Aquarius

This is an exciting and potentially profitable duo. However, Leo will have to get off her throne and forget about pushing this employee around. This is by no means a natural relationship, but if Leo will give up her passion to control and allow Aquarius the freedom to do it her way, there is big money to be had here. Leo will simply have to become a mature, understanding, and responsible manager, as well as hold back the criticism she is bound to have for the more frantic, unconventional Aquarius worker. These are two very different performers, but if Aquarius does bring home the dollars Leo will do about anything to make the pairing work.

Leo with Pisces

Who would suspect the strong, fierce, dramatic Lion could seek a vulnerable, sensitive, Pisces employee? The key is Pisces's highly creative and farsighted mind. This is exactly the kind of New World employee Leo loves to have on her stage. Pisces can create the kind of theatricality Leo thrives on, and Leo, under the surface, is the kind of encouraging, compassionate, and sympathetic boss Pisces must have. As long as Leo allows Pisces the freedom to operate, this could be a highly profitable, venture-capital type of duo. Big risks are taken here, but big money is possible in return.

Leo with Aries

These two have very similar personalities, making for a potentially exciting matchup. This mutual admiration society could be dynamic! It could also result in some majestic business decisions. This is a big-league duo with big plans. The problem could be with their egos: There can be no one boss. Only if each can agree to a 50/50 partnership will we see such spectacular commercial happenings.

Leo with Taurus

Both are often exactly the same things—the top job with all the power and the wealth. If they were even wise enough to agree to work together this could be a financial blockbuster of a pair and a big-league profit-making duo. But their personalities are so very different (slow plodding Taurus vs. perpetual motion Leo) and their egos are so strong and demanding that the result would be disastrously derisive. Each wants it her way and no compromise even seems likely.

Leo with Gemini

Try to make this work. It can spell big dollars with Leo directing Gemini. Leo will have trouble pinning down Gemini, but it can be done. There are a lot of similarities here and if Leo can get Gemini to be production-oriented, profitable results are on the horizon. The secret is for Leo to sell Gemini on the glamour side of the business and sweeten the Gemini pot with dollars. These two will also need a money manager to see that some of the profits are put back to work in the firm.

Leo with Cancer

This can be a good match for both if Leo makes the effort to be a more understanding boss. Cancer will have a very difficult time working for the demanding, high-pressure side of Leo and her world, but because she can be profitable it is worth Leo's time to protect Cancer and support her efforts in a low-key, more appreciative environment. Still this is a very tricky pairing (both need to be needed) and how stable it can be is doubtful. But if Cancer is a producer, Leo will do what she can to make her very comfortable. (Cancer, of course, could never be Leo's boss.)

ASTRAL FAX #5:
CHOOSING THE BEST PERSONAL SECRETARY

Whatever your sign, the astral manager needs a devoted, discreet, confidential "right-hand person": athe personal secretary.

How to know which one is "right" for you is the problem addressed here. Find your ideal businessmate from these qualities.

Aries: More of an entrepreneurial spirit than personal aide. Will pick and choose what jobs to do for you and will farm others out. Offers great creative support, advice, and fresh ideas but will be weak in office detail.

Taurus: An extremely competent, dependable, and serious employee. This is a strong sun sign personality who sometimes feels she knows more than you and knows how to do things better. If loss of some control in exchange for excellent job skills doesn't bother you, this sign is a valuable office manager.

Gemini: Not an easy personal employee to figure out, but an imaginative one. This sun sign will take orders then do things her way. Expect working relationship to be built around specific projects and not around personal closeness. Smart, creative, and capable but preferring to do it her way.

Cancer: Loyal, caring, and concerned. Solid work habits and a thoughtful organizer, with a good dose of creativity thrown in. Strong on personal skills, this is a trustworthy and dependable sign. Always there for you and always ready to do the job when asked.

Leo: A flamboyant, dramatic assistant who adds a bit of theater to your office operation. Prefers the big visible assignments to small jobs. Will need an assistant of her own to handle day-to-day details. Energetic front-office sun sign generating positive vibes.

Virgo: The ideal "get things done" sun sign. Prefers working behind the scenes to make life easier for you. Excellent work and scheduling skills. Virgo commands things to run smoothly. Smart and dependable, for many zodiac bosses this is the ideal personal secretary.

Libra: An independent spirit who will manage the office her way. Work will get done generally more smartly than you had imagined it to or ordered it to. You are buying her talent to perform her way, and frequently that difference adds value.

Scorpio: When a tough and demanding office personal secretary is called for you want Scorpio. It is like having another tough boss in the office. This is a big-picture personal secretary who delegates the chores. When a take-charge office attitude is needed you'll find it here.

Sagittarius: Fun, creative, and interesting is this personal secretary. Not born to detail, Sagittarius nevertheless finds unconventional ways to deal with work. Your customers and employees will enjoy Sagittarius in this friction-free environment.

Capricorn: Smart, hardworking, and serious, this personal secretary will be an excellent manager of the office. Also there is the additional attention to detail skills. Competence can be expected in any assignment this professional undertakes.

Aquarius: This independent sun sign works within her own guidelines. Capable and smart, but expect differences in how things will be done and when. With this personal secretary you are employing uniqueness and a different point of view, and there can be value in that. Plus customers and employees find this a very enjoyable individual.

Pisces: Loyalty and concern are important here. This is a sign that will work for you and do it your way. There is a strong personal relationship possible here as this devoted helper follows your wishes and your commands to the letter. Creativity is there also when you need it.

VI
Managing Virgo

August 24–September 23
Symbol: The Virgin
Ruling Planet: Mercury
Element: Earth
Motto: "The Power Behind the Throne"

A HISTORIC SAMPLING OF THE VIRGO WORKFORCE

Lauren Bacall	Ingrid Bergman
Joyce Brothers	Warren Buffett
Ray Charles	Agatha Christie
Patsy Cline	David Copperfield
Greta Garbo	Althea Gibson
Buddy Holly	Lyndon Johnson
Charles Kettering	Stephen King
Roger Maris	Christa McAuliffe
Slobodan Milosovic	Grandma Moses
Itzhak Perlman	Margaret Sanger
Oliver Stone	Margaret Trudeau
Leo Tolstoy	Raquel Welch

A Confidential Listing of Your
Virgo
Managers, Employees, and Colleagues

Name	Birth Date	Position

INTRODUCING VIRGO

This second Earth sign (first was Taurus), Mercury, who is the messenger and communicator of knowledge, rules Virgo. Virgo is Rodin's "The Thinker." This analytical sign will work methodically, seriously, and intelligently on every assignment you give him. Virgo's system of doing things sets a high standard in their work ethic and doing it their way is frequently the only way. A fact Virgo can prove if you ask him.

Clearly, spontaneity is not necessarily a strong suit with this sign and Virgo's confidence and certainty make him sometimes difficult to work with. But their dependability and smart, methodical approach makes them indispensable to any business. Difficult to know because of their high intelligence and sometimes-sharp tongue nevertheless when friendship or a working relation is established and respect is shared, you'll find Virgo a valuable and profitable companion.

Virgo Energy Profile

This is a deliberate, very thorough individual who works on restless nervous energy. Constantly active, Virgo is always busy, always doing, and rarely exists in a relaxed state. This is an efficient individual wasting no energy in getting a specific job done. This is by no means overwhelming energy, (nor is it spontaneous) but a body in continuous steady motion that is strictly task oriented.

Virgo Personality Profile

It is very difficult to get to know the so-called "modest" Virgo. You will notice right away that they possess impeccable manners and are well groomed. You will also notice that they can have solemn—almost cheerless and impersonal personalities, cool and reserved. (You'll find many unmarried Virgos.)

To a life of hard work born, Virgo is a practical, down to earth conservative who disdains a flashy lifestyle and those who live that way. (Fancy luncheons and relaxed vacations are not for him.) Virgos also disdain change. This is a creature of habit whose life has been planned down to the last detail. Uncomplicated, the Virgo is straightforward about life and no games, hypocrisy, or vanity will be tolerated.

Virgo is a mature overbearing adult whatever his age. He is serious, meticulous, and precise about everything he does. His obsession with detail makes him fussy, critical, fastidious, and small-minded. No doubt about it, Virgo is a perfectionist, and he expects everyone else to be.

Highly ethical, Virgo lives by a set of rules that no one must violate. Rules such as no smoking, no poor grammar, no messy rooms, be on time, work not play, and so forth. And he simply cannot understand why everyone does not believe in them and follow them. Everyone should be as faultless and as honorable as Virgo.

Virgo appears to be in control at all times—unemotional and unsentimental—and he rarely drops his guard, but internally he is the original worrier. Virgo worries about everything real or imagined. And because he appears on top of things, everyone else dumps personal problems on the Virgo. As a result, Virgo's insides are usually nervous, tense, and ulcerous. Why do Virgos listen? Why do they worry? Because they were also born to serve; they need to be needed, to care, and to help and they are concerned about everything and everyone—although you might never know it from their standoffish demeanor.

This self-imposed destiny to serve others has the negative effect of putting a boundary around Virgo's life. Capable of much more, Virgo nevertheless sees himself in a very limited role and rarely aspires to anything more or any role higher. This highly structured, task-oriented life is so binding that goals and dreams he could realize are not even attempted as Virgo settles very quickly into a one-track, one-dimension existence.

Regardless of Virgo's need to serve, he is not an easy person to care about in return. Basically efficient and demanding, Virgo has little time for frivolity or variety, and even less time to be tolerant of other lifestyles.

Virgo Intelligence Profile

No one is better at analyzing than Virgo. Slowly and carefully he can work out virtually any problem he is faced with. Questioning everything, wanting to know everything, he digs up every detail, for this is the zodiac's eternal student.

Acquiring knowledge and dispensing it are Virgo specialties. He is forever learning and forever improving. Here's a computer or a walking encyclopedia with all the pertinent information inside, forever both a teacher and a student. Virgo files away practical knowledge that has practical value. This is not an imaginative brain, but a serious, bare-facts brain.

Even though Virgo is a human file system of necessary information, his reticence to speak up can cover up his value. Frequently you will have to unlock the file system yourself. With Virgo so prepared, he frequently will have the answers or the job done before you even ask.

Virgo Communications Profile

Suspicious of big talkers, Virgo is an efficient, frank, and straightforward communicator. What he says is important. Expect no idle chatter. In fact, expect very little chatter of any kind unless solicited. When he does speak, however, he makes his point slowly but intelligently. Virgos are precise grammarians and express themselves with precision logic, even though it is difficult for them to express themselves at all. They are also excellent listeners, should the conversation or individual be worthy of their attention.

Virgo Diplomacy Profile

Preferring to work behind the scenes, Virgo has absolutely no interest at all in social diplomacy. Besides his native critical attitude would make him a disaster at this nevertheless necessary game. Only if a boss he respected required it of him, would he serve in this environment.

Virgo Money Profile

Money is not everything to Virgo, nor is it his primary motivation— doing a good job is. Still, Virgo expects to be paid well because of his superb work, and he are worth every dollar he is paid. However, because he is a workaholic, you will in fact never be paying him what he is really worth. Virgo also pays his workers only what they are worth, as well.

Virgo's financial picture is budgeted down to the last detail. He is also the ideal informed consumer. An expert money manager, this fiscal conservative can account for every penny spent, on the rare occasion he spends any.

Virgo's apparent greed is tied to his insecurity about the future. His fear of dependency drives him to hoard as much as he can to avoid having to accept the welfare of others.

Virgo Loyalty Profile

Sense of duty is extremely strong in Virgo. Virgo is in search of devotion to cause/company/individual/boss. Once committed, his attachment can transcend loyalty and verge on religious devotion. Virgos need to be loyal to someone or something in their lives, and they take this quest most seriously.

Virgo Work Habits Profile

Virgo is the sign of work and he can be the most capable employee you have—working by the rules, task-oriented, steady, reliable, giving unequalled service, never bothered by routine or detail, ready to take on the dirty work, obedient to the boss, neat, and precise. You get the picture (of course, the qualities also make him an ideal bureaucrat).

This is a dedicated, serious worker who performs best in a neat, highly organized atmosphere where he can keep on schedule without interruption. Motivated by doing his job better than anyone else, Virgo thrives in areas where his mental agility is put to the test. He also performs well in public service areas where, fulfilling his need to serve, his hand-earned achievements can have lasting social effects.

However, Virgos are most valuable as the number-two man to a corporate executive. The right-hand man, the executive secretary, the personal assistant—whatever the position is called—he is the boss's guide, advisor, order-taker, problem-solver, and behind-the-scenes aide de camp whose duty and loyalty are unquestioned (providing his boss has earned Virgo's respect to begin with). Always working in the background efficiently, productively and on schedule, Virgo carries out his responsibility to his boss with silent pride, making his boss's life much more effective and comfortable (and doing all the worrying for both of them). Because Virgo is best in supporting roles, however, his social and emotional characteristics are not fully developed. But the real damper is his critical nature. Virgo's perfectionist quality, although perfectly suited for most executive secretary functions can cause friction if turned against the boss. Virgo's demanding nature can get him ousted in short notice if he begins controlling the top man's way of doing business. For a healthy working relationship, Virgo must learn to couch his critical comments in terms of smart but friendly advice.

Virgo works according to a serious set of rules. He expects fellow workers to go by those rules. Clearly this is not an easy person to work with. But Virgos are invaluable, in the right position, so compromises are usually made.

Virgo Leadership Profile

Virgo is not prepared nor equipped to be a high-powered executive, nor is he looking for a leadership position. He knows where his real talents lie and he knows what his limitations are. He also doesn't have the ego drive or the desire for power to go after the top spot. He does however, expect to help build an empire—as long as he doesn't have to run it from the corner office.

Virgo's detail-oriented, organized mind is geared toward running the enterprise from behind the scenes (the power behind the throne) but not leading the way out front. His top level is second (or small group leader reporting to the top) and in that position he will make the leader look very, very good.

Should a Virgo ever fall into the number-one spot (should he not let destiny limit him or his dreams), he needs help filling in for his weaknesses. He will need another Virgo in the number-two position, as well as creative public relations and salespeople and power-welding assistants. Because Virgo is good at recognizing talent, he does have the ability to choose the kind of staff he needs to help him perform from a position he neither wants nor is made for. But with his sharp overbearing manner he is a very tough man to work for (perhaps impossible).

Virgo Success Potential Profile

To be successful, Virgo's life must be dedicated to serving:

- As the executive's right-hand man (executive secretary), where he is of value as a human encyclopedia, advisor, detail man, organizer, analyzer, and alter ego of the man on the throne.

- In the service of a righteous cause when Virgo brings his sense of caring and devotion to bear in helping others who can't help themselves.

Virgo feels he was placed on Earth to help, it's as simple as that; it's his duty and non-serving positions are totally unsuited to Virgo's nature. However, unless he can bend the rules and fit in with less-than-perfect people, Virgo's critical nature can be his undoing.

ZODIAC MANAGER'S VIRGO STRATEGY

- Somewhere in your organization you must have a Virgo/Virgos. This sign defines work, and everybody in the organization needs to see how a real pro does the job. This is a tough teacher and he will not suffer fools gladly, but the lessons learned from the workaholic role model will have a most beneficial effect on the quality of work done in your firm.

- It will be necessary to make it clear that as much as Virgo is valued and respected, you are the boss/supervisor. If you don't do this you will find many of your rules, standards, theories, goals, and performance scorecards slowly altered to meet Virgo's standards rather than yours. Although Virgo advice and counsel in such matters will undoubtedly be treasured, he must not contribute to a mutiny or an undermining of your position.

- In mapping out Virgo's career, promote him slowly and thoughtfully. Adapting to change is difficult for Virgo, and his fears of incompetence will come in to play if he feels he's in the wrong position. Recall, he is a thorough study so let him study his career track and proceed through it at a patience pace.

- Given Virgo's competence and self-reliance, your supervision will be minimal. This may give you the false hope that you can take frequent afternoons off and head for the golf course. Well, in fact you could if it weren't for one disturbing point: When you return you'll face the cold calculated evil eye of Virgo. Remember that he respects others who respect work, and you just fell a notch in his estimation of you. Play golf, but plan on re-earning some lost respect.

- Of all your employees, Virgo finds value in work, which is why he take it so seriously. The easiest way to lose Virgo is for those around him to take work frivolously. Work is a sacred calling, and Virgo will not tolerate anyone making light of it. Be certain that you place serious, like-minded employees around him to make the corporate position clear on the commitment to performance.

- Define Virgo's job clearly. Reduce any uncertainty, confusion, or chaos surrounding Virgo's specific responsibilities. Structure is vital to Virgo's performance, and rules must not be splintered or broken in getting the job done.

- Be prepared to repair any damage done to others by Virgo's critical nature. You won't be able to do much to stop it, but you can reduce the damage done by counseling with those who have felt the needle.

- Respect for you is the key to how well Virgo will perform. Virgo expects few things in return, for the duty of serving is paramount. Nevertheless, offering Virgo respect and security can win loyalty for life. Be very careful how you perform your job around Virgo, for the more Virgo admires you, the more Virgo will want to do for you.

- Allow space for Virgo to demonstrate his maximum talents and abilities. Take advantage of his work skills and see how far he can go to turn in a world-class performance. Virgo secretly wants to be your only employee so let him spread his wings and fly. Chances are you have underestimated his incredible work-oriented abilities. He's simply not like any other on the payroll.

- Always keep in mind Virgo's limitations as well as his talents. Don't put him in an unsteady situation that is poorly defined. Do put him in a situation where he can take the big picture and put it to work in the real world.

Virgo Most Profitable Location

This sun sign should be placed in a structured workspace near his boss. Virgo will immediately recognize it and forever keep it neat and tidy. Expect a clean desk at night. Virgo expects his office or those around him to be organized with everyone respectful of everyone else's work habits. Because Virgo is a workaholic, his office is run like an operating room: efficient and all business. Virgo will not tolerate interruptions and unkempt surroundings. He prefers a company with tradition located in a city.

Virgo Most Profitable Positions

Accountant
Assistant to President, Product Manager
Banker
Bank Worker
Bureaucrat
Chemist
Chiropractor
CIA Officer
Civil Servant
Claim Representative
Computer Expert
Counselor
Clergyman
Dentist
Dietician
Draftsman
Economist
Employment Counselor
Engineer
FBI Agent
Geologist
Historian
Home Economist
Internal Revenue Service Employee

Interpreter
Investment Manager
Labor Relations Specialist
Librarian
Life Scientist
Machinist
Market Analyst
Marketing Researcher
Medical Lab Technician
Meteorologist
Nurse
Occupational Therapist
Office Business Manager
Operations Research Analyst
Optometrist
Parole Officer
Pharmacist
Physical Therapist
Physicist
Physician

Plant Nursery Manager
Plumber
Psychiatrist
Publisher
Purchasing Agent
Retailer
School Guidance Counselor
Secretary
Social Worker
Soldier
Sports Official
Statistician/ Mathematician
Systems Analyst
Teacher
Technician
Traffic Manager (Industrial)
Trainer
Travel Agent
Underwriter
Veterinarian
Wholesaler

Virgo Job Skills Rating			
1 (Poor) to 5 (Excellent)			
Communications	3	Interpersonal Skills, Teamwork	3
Learning and Thinking Skills	5	Punctuality, Efficiency	5
Work Attitude	5	Loyalty	5
Creativity	3	Technology Skills	4
Problem-Solving	5	Self-Confidence	4
Decision-Making	5	Enthusiasm, Motivation	3
Money Management	5	Self-Management, Initiative	5
Flexibility	3	Honesty, Integrity	4
Accountability, Responsibility	5	Visionary	2
Planning Skills	5	Leadership	3
Details	5		

MANAGING VIRGO WORKING RELATIONSHIPS

In General

He doean't have many friends or acquaintances, because Virgo takes relationships very seriously with strict rules of behavior. But the few close friends he does have mean a great deal to him. On the other hand, Virgo has many he don't like—irresponsible Sagittarius, unreliable Gemini, moody Pisces, and showboating Leo—and so Virgo ends up staying aloof from many people. Virgo is also unsympathetic to those who are late, lazy, sloppy in dress, manners, or smarts, and who aren't always doing their best. This explains why so many Virgos go through life alone.

Those he serves get about as close to Virgo as anyone, but although Virgo gets to know them, it is seldom reciprocated. Respect for Virgo is about as close as it gets. Virgo wants to be closer, indeed he worries enough for all mankind, but few can match the standards he's set for lasting relationships. Virgo's friendly generosity, however, does extend to those who need Virgo's helping hand and sympathy.

Summary

Virgo Working Relationships		
PROFITABLE	RISKY	NON-PROFITABLE
Aries	Gemini	Virgo
Taurus	Leo	Cancer
Scorpio	Sagittarius	Libra
Capricorn	Aquarius	
	Pisces	

Bottom Line

Virgo with Virgo

These two will certainly understand the other's demanding nature right away, but it would be a battle of his rules verses your rules all the way. Any issue would be prime meat for argument. The competition would be ferocious with no winner—only two nasty temperaments. Virgo needs to serve a master or work for a respected boss. He does not need someone who thinks he's as good as he is—and *is* as good as he is.

Virgo with Libra

Virgo will feel that Libra breaks every business rule in the book: He's lazy, late, and indecisive, and he wastes time. They will agree on neatness but that's about it. Libra will drive the industrious, efficient Virgo up the wall. There's nothing here but Virgo anger and frustration.

Virgo with Scorpio

This is a capitalistic love match. These are two extraordinarily competent and profitable workaholics, and you can expect precision and efficiency when they are paired— with Scorpio as boss of course. This is the kind of manager Virgo has been looking for, a manager Virgo can respect and who is as conscientious as he is about every facet of the business. Scorpio likewise will find in Virgo his competent reliable alter ego. This may be the most productive duo in the zodiac.

Virgo with Sagittarius

A Virgo employee can make Sagittarius efficient and productive. Virgo's administrative skills and attention to detail are exactly what the globetrotting Sagittarius needs. However, if Virgo demands begin to restrict Sagittarius freedom, it's all over. There is a delicate balance that must be maintained to avoid constant friction.

Virgo with Capricorn

There isn't anything the responsible, industrious, dedicated Virgo assistant wouldn't do for a boss he respects and admires, and Capricorn is a boss who fits that bill. In this pairing, Capricorn has all the help he needs from an aide who is just as committed to the enterprise as he is. These are two very similar personalities except for one very fortunate difference: Capricorn wants to lead, and Virgo wants to serve. And Capricorn will be well served by this tough administrator, who will see to it that Capricorn orders are obeyed. Sometimes Virgo may come on too strong even to his Capricorn employer, but that is the small price you pay for having a perfectionist who makes it all work so smoothly.

Virgo with Aquarius

The strict, disciplinarian Virgo employee could certainly make organizational sense out of the frantic uncoordinated efforts of his Aquarius boss. In fact, Virgo's administrative skills are exactly what are needed here if Aquarius is to become efficient and profitable. But will Aquarius allow himself to be watched over this closely? Virgo is a tough perfectionist and this will never be to Aquarius's liking. But it is a productive pairing if Aquarius is willing to give up some of his freedom for a more effective enterprise.

Virgo with Pisces

The demanding Virgo vs. the undisciplined Pisces—two opposite personalities. Yet if Pisces is to be profitable, he needs this kind of partner. Virgo has the business skills to turn the highly imaginative Pisces into an efficient productive moneymaker. But the price the freedom-loving, sensitive Pisces pays may be too high. Virgo may hold the reins too tight and require too much of the unstructured, free-wheeling Pisces. And Virgo's critical nature can be damaging to the emotionally vulnerable Pisces. Still, if Pisces can adjust, and if Virgo can be more flexible, there is a chance for money here.

Virgo with Aries

There's great mutual respect and talent here. The natural tendency here, obviously, is for each to dominate. If these two dynamos agree to cooperate, the results could be staggering, provided detail-oriented people are hired to support this visionary pair.

Virgo with Taurus

Virgo is the perfect employee in Taurus's mind. These two work exactly alike: cautiously, thorough, paying attention to detail, etc. This is indeed a Taurus alter ego. Virgo will also have great respect for this boss, and that's what he needs to operate best. Excellent profit making twosome.

Virgo with Gemini

These two come from entirely different worlds. Personalities are likely to be at war frequently. But commercially, Gemini would find great value in the variety of routinized skills that Virgo brings to the relationship. In fact, Virgo can bring a needed long-term stability to an erratic Gemini venture. But will Virgo respect Gemini long enough to stay? And will Gemini accept Virgo's demanding rules for a successful business?

Virgo with Cancer

Cancer can no doubt use Virgo's superior business sense to make him commercially valuable. However, in process Cancer would become an emotional wreck trying to deal with all of Virgo's demanding rules for success. Only if Virgo decides poor Cancer needs his loyalty and devotion in this cold, cruel world could these two attempt a go at it. But chances are in the long run that Virgo will run out of patience and respect, and Cancer could be left comatose.

Virgo with Leo

Leo will have a solid detail-oriented perfectionist working for him. All those day-to-day problems Leo doesn't want to deal with, Virgo is pleased to tackle. But the easy-going Leo is going to have trouble with the overbearing and precise Virgo. And Virgo's going to have problems respecting a boss who relishes in showmanship tactics. The duo needs constant monitoring and compromise to be as profitable as we know it can be. The money involved makes it worth the effort.

ASTRAL FAX #6: THE DREAM TEAM

From choosing a committee, to an in-flight cabin crew, to an NBA starting five, to your office staff, the overall productivity of any team depends on how well the members complement one another. In other words, you need balance among the doers and the dreamers, the workers and the headers, the players and the coaches.

The astral manager has the advantage of knowing in advance what players to pick for each position and how they will fit in with each of the other players.

Whatever your task, here is your "perfect team"—according to the stars:

Let's begin with your visionary—the big picture guy who sees the whole enchilada. You can't go wrong with choosing Aries. Always far ahead of the pack, Aries is forever searching for new lands and ideas to conquer and always making a persuasive argument as to the rewards of conquest. Because of his passion to explore the widest of all possible horizons to find the new and daring means, you will rarely miss out on future opportunities, trends, and inventive solutions. And his dramatic energy generates the rallying cry around which the troops will flock willingly and enthusiastically.

Once Aries has seen the vision, it is time to hand it off to the nuts-and-bolts leader Taurus so the vision can be transformed to a practical mission. Taurus begins the process of translating the dream into reality by carefully planning what it will take to make the goal achievable. To give critical dimensions to this process of making the vision real, Taurus benefits from the earthy views of Capricorn and the creative imagination of Sagittarius. Although they come from two opposite ends of the spectrum, Capricorn and Sagittarius have enough respect for each other to allow for open discussion and debate that is friction-free. Taurus is the one, however, who filters through these diverse opinions, makes all final decisions, and puts financial numbers and scheduling dates to the project.

With Taurus deriving the strategic plans he now hands them off to Virgo for actual implementation. Virgo is a perfect workmanlike assistant for the Taurus boss and is content with his role behind the scenes and out of the spotlight. It is in this control room that Virgo doggedly attends to the day-to-day progress of the mission and reliably feeds back information directly to Taurus.

Need a gadfly? Sometimes having a critical independent voice can keep everyone else on their toes. Aquarius is your man. But carefully monitor his interaction with the other members of the team. He is a bit of a radical and a contraire. Filter his ideas and views through leader Taurus only. From the big picture to practical planning to sweating the details, this "Dream Team" plays championship caliber in any league.

VII

Managing Libra

September 24–October 23
Symbol: The Scales
Ruling Planet: Venus
Element: Air
Motto: "I'll Give You A Definite Maybe"

A HISTORIC SAMPLING OF THE LIBRA WORKFORCE

Gene Autry	Brigitte Bardot
Art Buchwald	Truman Capote
Chubby Checker	Michael Douglas
F. Scott Fitzgerald	Janet Gaynor
George Gershwin	Lillian Gish
Bryant Gumbel	Helen Hayes
Rita Hayworth	Lee Iacocca
Donna Karan	Buster Keaton
Annie Liebovitz	Groucho Marx
Martina Navratilova	Emily Post
Eleanor Roosevelt	Ed Sullivan
Margaret Thatcher	Barbara Walters

A Confidential Listing of Your
Libra
Managers, Employees, and Colleagues

Name	Birth Date	Position

INTRODUCING LIBRA

An Air sign, Libra is ruled by Venus, goddess of love in mythology and known for creating harmony. With the Scales as the symbol for this sign, Libras are known for seeking balance. In this search, Libra becomes adept at weighing both sides of the problem to find the right way. The search for the pros and the cons on all subjects can lead to indecision and procrastination as well as total understanding.

Libras have a great love for life and cherish healthy relationships. These diplomats hope to create a world of understanding and unity. There is, however, a critical side to Libra that emerges when her points of view are doubted. Also, in Libra's search for fairness and justice, she sometimes becomes too judgmental of others.

In business, Libra's search for the "truth" and her ability to create harmony are valuable prizes to possess.

Libra Energy Profile

Plays hard. Rests hard. A daydreamer one moment, active the next. Lazy one moment, on the go the next. Restless activity is followed by a long leisurely lunch. Libra's energy can be seen in these extremes, although she strives to reach a healthy, middle-of-the-road balance. When she reaches that balance, Libra will appear to lack drive. She will appear to be daydreaming with a poised, serene, above-it-all manner. This is the calm outward pose she's been working for. But this balance is rarely achieved or retained for long, so the stop-and-go Libra is the one you most frequently encounter.

Libra Personality Profile

Party animal, charming host, and sought-after guest, Libra desires to live the good life. The cheerful, witty, and elegant individual you are about to meet has an aura of grace, beauty, and poise, reflecting a sophisticated image: warm, calm, and collected, refined, courteous, and attractive. Libras popularity and winning manner draw many friends and admirers. Libra's have a great admiration for beauty and "culture" and those are necessary elements in her life. To look at Libra, you wouldn't think she had a worry in the world, not this easygoing romantic who is such delightful company. You'd never believe for a moment that anything on Earth could phase her. But alas, underneath there is considerable turmoil. The fact is that this outward appearance of harmony and balance we see is exactly what Libra is after, but unfortunately for most Libras it ends up a facade and a pose, nothing ingrained. Indeed, many of them will struggle internally all their lives for truth, meaningful equilibrium, and peace. The symbol for Libra is the scale, and to keep a level-headed, emotionally tempered happy medium life is the Libra's lifelong quest. But scales tip two ways and are rarely in balance, so you will also discover a world of contradictions and ambivalence. Generosity or greed, peacemaker or argumentative, kind or cold, pleasure or pain, up and down, half the time one way and half the time the other—then suddenly balance! Until the scales are tipped again.

This out-of-balance Libra loses the sense of who she is or what is meant to be accomplished. Libra will blame herself for her identity crisis, for her inability to find the truth or inner peace with her inadequate sense of self she becomes self critical and self-punishing. She has failed to achieve perfection and the high standards she set for herself. In this state Libra can retreat into a solution of relying on others to give her a sense of worth. This can create a Libra who temporarily lives by what others think of her.

Because this Libra is aiming to please, she is gullible and easily influenced by what is popular. Libra rarely makes judgements free and clear of what will please the crowd. Applause and flattery are her downfall.

What else can be said about the complex, contradictory Libra? She is intelligent, immensely creative because she is a perfectionist, she is sometimes shy and reticent, afraid to say the wrong thing she believes in fair play and pull for the underdog, and she is an idealist. She wants the beautiful life without inner turmoil. She wants to avoid and bypass the real world struggle and live in a romantic atmosphere.

Finally, with so much charm, talent, and creativity, it is truly unfortunate that Libras spend any time at all out of balance sabotaging themselves. This is what makes them erratic, insecure, and personalities. But the balanced Libra who asserts her true self and takes control of her own life is a masterful individual who is capable of dazzling those inside and outside the organization. Negative thoughts and emotional uncertainties must not eat up Libra's great business talent. The healthy rule of thumb for Libra must be "the less time you spend worrying about yourself the better" or, in other words, "Lighten up, Libra!"

Libra Intelligence Profile

Remember that the Scales are the symbol for Libra, and that's a good place to start understanding Libra intelligence. First, this is not a fast mind but it is a smart one. It takes time for Libra to learn and decide. Now here's where the balancing scales come in: Libras are superb at seeing both sides of an argument (a judge's mentality, for example) and because they consider the pros and cons of every situation they are excellent troubleshooters and negotiators. This judicious arbitrator is analytically gifted at sorting out all the facts to make her decision. However, because she is so good at understanding both sides, Libra can do more fence-sitting than decision-making, resulting in Libra indecisiveness. At her analytical best, Libra can be logical and perceptive. Her powers of analysis are strong in her quest for the perfect solution and the right judgment. Libra's experience gives her street smart knowledge on a wide range of subjects. But perhaps one of her strongest suits is her creativity, which is capable of building amazing scenarios and events.

Caution: Libras are also intuitive and are capable of substituting hunches for reality, understanding the big picture too quickly, and glossing over detail. This may be due to their inner desire of taking the easy way out. And many times they prefer daydreaming to thinking. Beware of their tendency to be glib when perspective and dimension are required.

Libra Communications Profile

This is that rare combination of a highly verbal individual who is a superb listener (listening to all sides of the discussion is how she learn s everything there is to learn about a given subject). Libra has mastered communication skills and uses them like a professional. Verbal manipulation is an art form here. A charming persuader, a friendly debater, glib, and with excellent powers of expression, Libra can influence seemingly without arguing as she subtly persuades you to her side.

Frequently, however, when Libra is asked for an answer, solution, or advice, be prepared for a lecture so that every angle is covered and all sides are represented.

Libra Diplomacy Profile

Libra's desire for personal peace and equilibrium, combined with her outward calm charm and grace, make her an absolutely perfect diplomat. Libra loves to entertain and she knows all the social graces; she's courteous, well-mannered, tactful, witty, pleasing, and sociable. There should be no ruffled feathers at a Libran occasion. Libra is overwhelmingly thoughtful of and concerned for her guests and will do everything possible to make them happy. Libra's tendency to be indecisive (fence sit) is a positive trait in diplomatic circles, and you could not find a more judicious, civil, and concerned host.

Libra Money Profile

Libra is an extravagant spender! This is a real lover of luxury and the beautiful life. In fact, beauty and luxury rule Libra's life. How can this jet-setter make the kind of money she needs to live so high? Believe it or not, she trades on her charm and her appearance. And how can she get away with simply that? Because Libra is also the luckiest sign in the zodiac. Libra attracts money without trying and without making much effort. Still Libra needs a money manager to enforce some conservative spending, to set a budget, and to harness-large scale speculative investments to protect those lucky dollars from running out.

Libra Loyalty Profile

Libra wants desperately to be loyal and wants it returned. In fact, this is one of the highest priorities in her life. She needs to be a part of a fiercely devotional relationship or group. To a great extent, Libra measures her self-esteem by how others relate to her. Loyalty is the absolute confirmation she can receive that says, "She's terrific." Once loyalty has been established she expects it to last a lifetime. Libra is too fragile to handle getting burned by someone who was that close.

Libra Work Habits Profile

This is not a physical laborer. Definitely not! Libra is attracted to jobs requiring brainstorming or artistic and creative skills fulfilling her need to create beautiful experiences or things. (In fact, you will find Libra's work much more productive where their work environments are extremely attractive as well.)

Libra has a good mind (ideas and analysis are their strengths) but abhors detail and nine to five at the desk. Content to think or dream about ideas, she can fail to carry them through to their logical conclusion, and she quickly becomes bored by long-range tasks. Getting a Libra's attention and interest is a real trick. And even after you have given her an assigned task, when out of balance, she can look for the easy way out and give it over to someone else or use someone else's skills to get it done.

Libra is attracted to "people jobs" and works much better in non-competitive, cooperative groups. Here she can perform extremely well as discussion leader, peacemaker, and mediator. An excellent tactician, Libra can bring out all sides of an issue and direct the discussion to a fair and agreeable group solution.

Because people should always be a part of what Libra does, the customer relations area is a particularly appropriate position for her. Out-front positions requiring diplomacy and promotion are Libra strong suits. But above all, avoid putting her under pressure or tension. Without a tension-free and harmonious atmosphere, Libra can't perform.

Clearly, Libra's work habits have limitations. She is a real specialist and does not perform well unless both the job and the environment are ideally suited to her. Libra simply does not fit in to most job descriptions.

Libra also requires a boss who is a real professional when it comes to motivating people—someone who can take time with a Libra and get her to commit herself to the total task, to get her to assume responsibility, and to speak up for what she really thinks is the right way to do the job. Unfortunately the inner concerns Libra brings to work are very difficult to direct and motivate. But a boss will profit by investing the time and money necessary to create an environment in which Libra can be her charming, conciliatory, and creative best. Keep Libra busy, avoid time for self, and balance those scales, and you have created a condition in which Libra can thrive.

Libra Leadership Profile

Simply put, Libras are rarely leaders. There can be an occasional Libra superstar who has it all together and has become a billionaire entrepreneur. Libra works best in groups or in partnerships, but just does not possess the variety of organizational and administrative skills required to lead a business. In fact, when out of balance, Libra has an almost anti-business personality—indecisive, noncompetitive, daydreaming, no profit-making orientation. Also, Libra wants to be popular and appreciated. Leaders need to be aggressive and thick-skinned. Those moments when Libra is in balance, however, you would swear you are in the company of a world class charismatic leader. And the truth is, if Libra could be like that all the time she would be a leader.

Libra Success Potential Profile

Libra possesses considerable charm, creativity, and, let's not forget, luck. Although she is not a born capitalist, she does have the potential to succeed financially and artistically in highly specialized professions. Her ability to succeed will depend on her choosing a direction, developing the self-confidence needed to reach her goal and collect her reward (the recognition and undying respect of others). This formula can help Libra acquire the good life she so desperately wants to lead. Also, the more her work occupies her time, the less time she has to worry about herself and the more in balance she will be.

Libra can also be successful in group leadership roles and in the area of social causes. Fighting for freedom and equality is a challenge Libra gladly takes on. Fighting for society's underdogs is in a sense fighting for herself.

The road to professional success can be a rocky and chancy one for Libra, but, because of her uncanny good fortune, charm, and creativity, she can do surprisingly well, even though business isn't really made for this independent complex spirit.

ZODIAC MANAGER'S LIBRA STRATEGY

- Most importantly, understand you are dealing with at least two personalities here: balanced and unbalanced. As management, you must find ways to keep Libra balanced as much as possible. Make sure the job fits the Libra personality. Next, provide freewheeling office space and team-oriented colleagues. Finally, some kind of "safety net" must be in place when Libra takes an emotional tumble. Libra requires an excellent supervisor with time to spend. The rewards for keeping Libra balanced can be ample.

- Libra's career chart is one of the narrowest in the zodiac. Careers off the chart will only serve to unbalance Libra's scales. Where analytical skills and creativity are required you've tipped the scales in her and your favor.

- Don't let Libra's fragile nature keep you from putting her in challenging situations. Libra has the skills to create magic moments and dazzling products/services. In fact, she is capable of outshining everyone else in the organization. So don't protect her too much or you'll never see this "shoot for the moon" side that Libra can accomplish better than anybody.

- Libra has a strong sense of justice and fairness. She trusts and needs to be trusted. Do not place this individual in a situation that would compromise her principles. Social causes are important to Libra, and she doesn't take to criticism of "doing good work" for others. This is a concerned and compassionate sign and this aspect of Libra must also feel comfortable in your organization.

- If/when you discover that your particular Libra is more unbalanced than balanced, chances are you'll be wasting your time (and hers) trying to correct it. There will be those Libras who just do not fit in with the structure of today's organization and there is little that can be done. This Libra simply can't, and never will, work according to your schedule. Also beware of the high standard Libra. You need to know if she believes in what your organization does and how it does it. If her principles don't match yours, nothing profitable will come of your relationship.

- Libras work very well in partnership. They are team players and delight in participating in a wide range of team activities. See that she is performing in part of a group for maximum productivity. Likewise, you can recognize an unbalanced Libra if she prefers to work close. This is both unhealthy and unproductive.

- Libra is not a quick worker. Expect Libra assignments to take time, but also expect them to be impeccably carried out. With a perfectionist mentality, this searcher for truth and justice will never turn out second-rate or poorly thought-out work. Even a deadline will not help.

- Do not hide Libra in the company's back room. Show her off and let her show off the company in return. This is an excellent frontperson with a sunshine charm that will make you and your company look big time. This is a superb employee to take to major affairs and meetings.

- Libras are excellent sounding boards for your ideas and thoughts. Let Libra in on what you and the organization are thinking. She will listen well, analyze well, and give you a logical and intelligent report on what she thinks. Libra's ability to distance herself from most issues makes her an invaluable non-partisan observer and commentator on what's going on in the world around her.

- Never be surprised when Libra suddenly goes out of balance. She is her own worst enemy, and her self-criticism and self-doubt are of her own making. All you can do is try to counter this with admiration and respect. Eventually the scales will again balance.

Libra Most Profitable Positions

Actor	Interior Designer/ Decorator	Public Relations Executive
Architect	Interpreter	Radio/TV Personality
Art Dealer	Judge	Real Estate Broker
Artist	Labor Relations Specialist	Retailer
Beautician	Lawyer	Salesperson
Collector	Lobbyist	Secretary
Commercial Artist	Merchandiser	Singer
Counselor	Model	Social Worker
Creative Idea Man	Musician	Systems Analyst
Dancer	Negotiator	Traffic Manager (Industrial)
Dietician	New Product Developr	Travel Agent
Diplomat	Personnel Employee	Union Activist
Entertainer	Philosopher	Writer
Fashion Designer	Photographer	
Horticulturist		

Libra Most Profitable Location

Libra is extremely sensitive to her surroundings (both physical and human), and if she is not in harmony with her environment she cannot function. She needs a pleasing, most attractive, dramatic atmosphere where money has not been spared and filled with the most tasteful and very best furnishings available. Her own work area should be open and accessible. Libra is a team worker and she needs space to interact with others. Libra also needs the support of others to work at her analytical and creative best, so her team should be located near or within this open territory. Only if Libra is in harmony and balance with the people and the office can she perform profitably.

Libra Job Skills Rating

1 (Poor) to 5 (Excellent)

Communications	4	Interpersonal Skills, Teamwork	4
Learning and Thinking Skills	5	Punctuality, Efficiency	4
Work Attitude	4	Loyalty	4
Creativity	4	Technology Skills	3
Problem-Solving	5	Self-Confidence	4
Decision-Making	3	Enthusiasm, Motivation	4
Money Management	3	Self-Management, Initiative	4
Flexibility	4	Honesty, Integrity	4
Accountability, Responsibility	4	Visionary	3
Planning Skills	4	Leadership	3
Details	5		

MANAGING LIBRA RELATIONSHIPS

In General

Libras are people persons, confidants to the world, popular, generous, and good company. Libras find friendships everywhere and people like them, but they prefer to move in the best social circles where they, with little effort, attract prestigious acquaintances. Although Libra can be the life of the party and so much fun to be with, she is ultra-sensitive to what others think about her. Easily hurt, Libra tries to be extra nice to people and as a result she can be pushed around and manipulated. The need to be loved and accepted is very strong with Libra, and she can rush into the wrong relationships quickly and without thinking. To keep emotionally healthy, Libra needs the applause and encouragement of friends. Libra also returns the favor and will listen for hours to a friend in need.

You will also see the other extreme: the shy, retiring Libra. This is the part of her personality that backs off for fear of being wrong, getting hurt, or not winning the applause. And this is a condition existing inside every Libra—her outward appearance to the contrary.

Summary

Libra Working Relationships		
PROFITABLE	RISKY	NON-PROFITABLE
Taurus	Capricorn	Libra
Cancer		Aries
Leo		Gemini
		Virgo
		Scorpio
		Sagittarius
		Aquarius
		Pisces

Bottom Line

Libra with Libra

As coworkers in a creative group, these two have value. But they will probably need a motivation unless one decides to direct the team and actually sticks to it long enough to see results. The chance of profitability here is doubtful, however, because this is a duo that would prefer to follow their own dreams or passions of the moment and not a business manager's.

Libra with Scorpio

Scorpio is capitalism defined. Libra needs careful coaxing to even become involved in the capitalist race. Scorpio will simply have no time for someone she considers as commercially out of step as Libra. Libra offers the efficient, productive, and driven Scorpio nothing at all in a business relationship.

Libra with Sagittarius

Chances are Libra won't even try to keep with the self-assured, individualistic Sagittarius. Libra will be her greatest fan and a worshiper, but otherwise she offers no commercial value to the Sagittarius. Sagittarius simply does not have the time to help what she will consider to be an ineffective personality. Libra needs understanding and guidance, not avoidance.

Libra with Capricorn

Capricorn's managerial skills can make Libra's entrance into the pressure-filled commercial world possible if Libra is productive. Libra is a breed apart from the capitalist, career-oriented, profit-making Capricorn. However, her analytical skills can be profitable to the always-learning Capricorn. If Capricorn can temper her demanding, do-it-my-way nature (and she'll do almost anything to make money) and carefully manage Libra's skills in a productive way this can be a productive pairing. However, it is not a natural relationship but one based solely on a Capricorn need, and if Libra doesn't produce it will be all over (except for Libra's bruises, which last a long time).

Libra with Aquarius

Libra searches for balance and harmony. Aquarius pursues the future. These are opposites! Aquarius investigates, uncovers, changes, rearranges, and explores; Libra is trying to piece together the puzzle putting it into a peaceful existence. This may be the original odd couple. In fact, Libra could suffer emotional bruises in this pairing. Aquarius is simply too frenetic and too revolutionary for the emotionally struggling Libra, who wants to be left alone in a calm and protected room.

Libra with Pisces

The indecisive Libra and the indecisive Pisces are handily a productive duo. These two aren't really born for commercial world and, in fact, have constructed worlds of their own away from that harsh competitive arena.

Their business skills just aren't strong enough to give them an advantage whether alone or together. They are emotionally and personally compatible, but they just aren't disciplined enough to be profitable.

Libra with Aries

The fast-paced, aggressive Aries has very little time for the less active, dream-oriented Libra. We find virtually nothing in common between these two. In fact, it would pose a potential disaster for Libra to try and run in the fast lane with Aries.

Libra with Taurus

The Taurus boss could use the creativity of a Libra employee. And the Taurus boss is patient with and understanding of the less-disciplined and less task-oriented Libra personality. On the other hand, Libra will find comfortable but assertive guidance from Taurus. But Libra will have to produce eventually, or Taurus will call a quick end to it. Taurus requires profits at some point. If Libra can deliver, this is about the best commercial relationship she can find.

Libra with Gemini

Libra wouldn't even get into the same race with Gemini. Nor would brilliant dynamic Gemini even appreciate the creative Libra dream world. These two will find nothing in common, nor offer anything to the other. These are two totally different personalities—with two totally different business attitudes.

Libra with Cancer

Cancer and Libra can work very well together. Creatively talented, their personalities also mesh and they will understand each other's vulnerability very well. With proper commercial guidance the two should turn out profitable ideas. Don't expect electricity. And don't force them to move too fast. Just keep them on target and they should deliver.

Libra with Leo

Although Libra's actual commercial value to Leo is suspect, boss Leo may decide her employee's charm to be just the ticket to promote her operation and to keep her clients very happy. These are two great frontwomen, and their good life personalities are wonderfully similar. There is no routine or detailed office work here, just the exciting big picture and the decidedly theatrical side of business.

Libra with Virgo

Virgo will feel that Libra breaks every business rule in the book: She's lazy, late, and indecisive, and she wastes time. They will agree on neatness, but that's about it. Libra will drive the industrious efficient Virgo up the wall. There's nothing here but Virgo anger and frustration.

Astral Fax #7: "Carrots"

What do you offer the horse after a good workout? A carrot, of course. So what kind of carrots do you offer to business professionals you want to hire or employees you want to keep or promote? The following list, sign by sign, reveals what carrots tip the scales when it comes to "buying" the skills of the talented:

Aries: Highly visible job with powerful title and free time to create.

Taurus: Mucho bucks and expensive toys.

Gemini: Front job "educating" others on the business.

Cancer: Security and principles.

Leo: The spotlight.

Virgo: Increased responsibility.

Libra: A caring concerned team.

Scorpio: Power.

Sagittarius: Future-oriented projects.

Capricorn: Money and power.

Aquarius: Independent projects.

Pisces: Creative freedom in a secure, supportive environment.

VIII

Managing Scorpio

October 24–November 22
Symbols: The Scorpio, The Eagle,
The Serpent, The Phoenix
Ruling Planet: Pluto
Element: Water
Motto: "L'état c'est moi"

A Historic Sampling of the Scorpio Workforce

Spiro Agnew	Fanny Brice
Pat Buchanan	Christopher Columbus
Ruby Dee	Dale Evans
Sally Field	Indira Gandhi
Bill Gates	Charles de Gaulle
Whoopi Goldberg	Grace Kelly
Hedy Lamar	Dennis Miller
Margaret Mitchell	Jane Pauley
Pablo Picasso	Helen Reddy
Roy Rogers	John Phillip Sousa
Marlo Thomas	Ted Turner
DeWitt Wallace	Henry Winkler

A Confidential Listing of Your Scorpio
Managers, Employees, and Colleagues

Name	Birth Date	Position

INTRODUCING SCORPIO

This Water sign is ruled by the dark planet Pluto, in mythology the God of the underworld, representing deep transformation. This most passionate and most powerful sign in the zodiac possesses enormous strength as it secretly moves toward control. Intensely competitive, this sign rarely concedes defeat and, if defeated, expect revenge.

Scorpio is serious about life and lightweight, superficial opinions, solutions, or people are treated harshly. With a magnetic personality, this sun sign can attract dedicated followers and true believers. Acutely intuitive and tenaciously committed, Scorpios do not give up, whether pursuing a complex situation or a sexual partner.

Scorpios are best when dealing with affairs of the greatest worldly importance. The only acceptable challenge for them is to address issues of the greatest magnitude.

Scorpio Energy Profile

You are about to encounter the most powerful sign in the universe. First, there are those hypnotic piercing eyes that seem to cut right through you (a look that kills). Then, there is the unrivaled energy, the highest energy level of all signs, yet sheathed in a cool, serious, and detached facade. Finally, there is the fascinating magnetism that can draw you to him. Scorpios define poised power with explosive potential, and against the mature Scorpio there is little competition in this area. Scorpio throws his boundless energy into every project he commits himself to. But he is also quite capable of changing direction in an instant, leaving all his previous accomplishments behind. Thriving on pressure, this intensely charged individual needs moments of escape and quiet meditation to keep him emotionally sane. However, even during this "meltdown" you can detect Scorpio's potential high-octane energy level. Indeed, this is a carefully controlled bundle of raw power waiting to erupt at the desired and perfectly orchestrated moment. (Or as Scorpio Teddy Roosevelt said, "Speak softly but carry a big stick.")

Scorpio Personality Profile

Much about Scorpio is mysterious, and he prefers it that way. He's psychic, intuitive, and presumably able to see the whole truth in one quick, penetrating glance. In fact, he's alleged to be able to unlock the deepest secrets of the universe as well as possess hypnotic powers. Refusing to let anyone get close to him, he thrives on privacy and secrecy and frequently uses secrecy as a weapon. Is it possible that he needs to appear inscrutable because he is emotionally vulnerable?

A perfectionist, Scorpio appears to be in total control and the master of his physical and emotional being. This is an egomaniac who can use his eyes, voice, brain, body, or passion to manipulate anyone. Driven and obsessed, Scorpio lives a self-willed and self-directed life and is persistently determined to get his way.

Scorpio can also totally change his mood as the occasion warrants. Kind, compassionate, and friendly, he can also turn himself into a stubborn, resentful, suspicious, and even cruel loner. (In fact, this evil, masochistic streak is not uncommon in Scorpio.) This sun sign is a law unto himself and possesses the greatest psychological strength of any sign in the zodiac. Shrewd and manipulative, he lives his intense life to the fullest.

With all these dark and mysterious elements to Scorpio, he needs to widen his vision and relax his egocentric existence. But it is difficult for Scorpio to lose control. However, even in control he swerves sharply from left to right—from a devoted sympathetic family man, he can quickly turn possessive, jealous, and aggressive, revealing Scorpio's deep, passionate nature and his intense sexual appetite. Or he can be excellent company, enjoying life before, again, suddenly turning it all off and abruptly departing in another direction. This tendency to simply cut in and out of various moods also extends to cutting in and out of various events in his life (marriage, jobs, locations), and it is part of his nature to change his master plan whenever he wants to.

Scorpio is born with immense power, and his anger can be unrivaled. This is the sun sign of passion, which rules his life. (Yet for all his passion, he dislikes the show of simple emotion in others.) He is always potentially dangerous, because he can will himself to do whatever necessary to get his way. It is this negative side that can wash away his incredible magnetism, and he must be careful not to let this happen, for his personal magnetism is indispensable in his drive for control and power. When he turns it on, Scorpio magnetism can take him anywhere.

Scorpio Intelligence Profile

This is a fascinating and most unusual mind. Scorpio are said to have the mental ability to control people around them, through mind control! How's that for openers?

Then, of course, there is the unquenchable need to increase their body of knowledge every day. Even down to exploring the mysteries of life, Scorpio absorbs facts quickly and he is always searching and probing for the kind of information that enhances his power. By the time this sun sign reaches the top, he will have learned everything he needed to know to operate with perfection. He will have read every book, listened to every expert, and analyzed and examined every aspect of the job industry.

Although you can always call on the Scorpio mind for its inexhaustible supply of facts and figures, it is also an active, imaginative, and creative brain full of new ideas, new concepts, and inventions. Scorpio is a discoverer, an investigator, the one who finds all the profitable answers, a commercially valuable encyclopedia adding volumes daily to his impressive existing set of knowledge.

Scorpio also possesses the kind of mind that loves to play games. Like a master chess player, he makes his intellectual moves carefully and secretly, quietly calculating his victory in any debate or encounter. He also has the mind of a gambler, constantly playing the odds. Add to all this intense intellectualism Scorpio's brilliant intuition and mystical perception, and it's hard to find a mind that can challenge him. Beware, however: Occasionally his passions get the best of him and his emotions can overwhelm his intellect.

Scorpio Communications Profile

Communicating verbally and with his body and his eyes, Scorpio can be brutally frank, sarcastic, and outspoken. Blunt and curt, he does not indulge in idle chatter. Nor will Scorpio tolerate emotional language or gossip, and forget flattery.

However, in general expect Scorpio reaction to be at a bare minimum. He'll not give away his feeling or thoughts verbally or physical. His face is an inscrutable masking of his inner thoughts.

In general, it's not very easy talking to a Scorpio because it's so difficult to read how he's taking your remarks. However, if the content of your remarks is certifiably intelligent, he will give you time because he will be registering every word (this is a major way he learns so much, by listening).

Scorpio is a smart, efficient conversationalist and a communications control artist. He knows how to get what he wants out of a colleague. Short, smart sentences are the best way to get through to Scorpio.

Scorpio Diplomacy Profile

Frank, suspicious, efficient, egocentric, manipulative, unemotional, obsessed with self, possessive, perfect, unbending—put all these Scorpio traits together and you've got the world's worst diplomat—unless! Scorpio decides he needs to be diplomatic to win a power play. Even with this naturally negative diplomacy quotient, if Scorpio wills himself in a specific direction (i.e., superb host), he can reverse his entire personality and become anyone he wants. But remember, he will only agree to be diplomatic and succeed at it if he has decided he needs to in order to accumulate even greater power.

Scorpio Money Profile

Scorpio is obsessed with money—and obsessed with profit. But only in the sense that he is obsessed with the power and prestige money can bring.

Then, digging deeper, we find two very different approaches to the use of money. There is the one Scorpio who is obsessed with spending. This Scorpio loves creature comforts and fills his home and office with the best that money can buy. The intense and hungry nature of this Scorpio makes it impossible for him to satisfy all his big-league needs. However, this spender and speculator does know enough to stop just short of bankruptcy and total loss of control over his affairs.

The other Scorpio can endure years of poverty if necessary to reach his position of top earner. Even at the peak he desires only a few expensive possessions. This Scorpio has great disdain for big spenders, looking at them as simpletons who find pleasure in vulgar ways.

In general, however, Scorpio is so good at the game called capitalism that he makes enough money whichever type he happens to be. And as a venture capitalist, in particular, he can really excel. And fortunately the big spending Scorpio is a big money-maker, as well.

Scorpio Loyalty Profile

Although he has no patience for the superficial, Scorpio is extremely devoted to and possessive of those few he loves (usually, this consists only of his family and a few friends). He is loyal to productive, like-minded, fellow workers and employees, and he will be very generous in his loyalty as long as they continue to measure up to his high standards.

Scorpios, themselves, demand 100-percent devotion (of the "thou shalt have no other Gods before me" variety) and they do attract a solid crowd of fiercely loyal, true believers. However, there is a larger crowd of envious resentful enemies and just plain frightened folk who stay miles away. Yet, for the devoted friend, Scorpio has been known to lay down his life to protect his in moments of crisis.

Scorpio is also known to help those in need and is drawn, in particular, to those who need redemption or need to be saved, provided that have been proven to have "worth" as defined by Scorpio.

Scorpio Work Habits Profile

The highly competitive Scorpio has a considerable inventory of work-oriented skills to perform the toughest jobs you can find. His "all work no play" attitude is exactly what the capitalist ordered. He simply must be productive 24 hours a day at the most important job there is, and no inter-ruptions will be tolerated. His backbreaking schedule will not allow any interference in his highly structured day. So certain is he of his problem-solving abilities that any criticism of his efforts is simply not tolerated— particularly criticism that insults his intelligence.

This is the real workhorse of the zodiac. Intense, tenacious, determined, dedicated, and with a passionate sense of purpose, Scorpio thrives on pres-sure and deadlines. His intelligence, self-confidence, and naturally prob-ing curiosity qualify him for virtually any professional position. He'll get the job done whatever it is. This is truly Mr. Productivity. This is the man with the brilliant ideas that turn big profits. So you're going to run right out and put an ad in the paper for a Scorpio employee, right? Well, like every-thing else, this is too good to be true. Here's the catch: Scorpio is a superb worker, which is true. But he's just passing through on his way to fulfilling his own master plan.

Scorpio knows the rules of business better than anyone does, and he plays the game superbly well. Even though he is basically very difficult to get along with (he considers himself better than anyone else) and he will resent being bossed around, he knows what side his bread is buttered on, and to get to the top he'll do what he's told. But he's only working long enough to learn how to boss you. This is a goal-oriented worker with a strong sense of direction and that direction is upward. Scorpio is truly the "master of his fate and the captain of his soul." He is obsessed with doing his job well to get the raises, promotions, and recognition he deserves. As he engineers his career towards the position of ultimate power, true, he is not naturally people-oriented nor a pleasant staff or line worker, but he can will himself to be to get where he wants.

Scorpio is an unrivaled employee who will perform better than anyone else so that you will reward him and send him up to the next rung on the professional ladder. If he is rewarded as he expects, you can expect 150-percent loyalty to the organization and its goals.

Expect undercurrents of tension, however, because no matter how obliging Scorpio may try to be on his way up, he is, in fact, engaged in a power struggle, which is bound to inflict bruises all the way to the executive suite. Also, don't be surprised if Scorpio suddenly stops and turns his life around 180 degrees. This sun sign is so sure of himself that he is capable of leaving a very successful employment and strike out in a totally new field. Remember, at the core, his own passion and destiny is directing and motivating him.

Scorpio Leadership Profile

More world leaders, prominent politicians, and CEOs are Scorpios than any other sign, which is because Scorpio equals power! Which is what Scorpio is after. Cool under pressure, with an unflappable tower of strength, this brilliant manipulator is a first-class executive (and more often than not, chief executive). This is commander-in-chief material capable of dispensing orders efficiently and intelligently. This is a battlefield general whose hypnotic appeal can motivate his dedicated, loyal troops to obey his every command. This is an impressive, magnetic leader who is in absolute control and can draw out of his followers everything they are capable of giving. Forget the competition. This is the winner. Demanding, with great attention to detail, this is the man who makes the decisions, and the more challenging the better.

As your boss, don't try flattery and never try to top him. You can also forget about deception because he knows when you are telling him the truth and when you're not. His intuition and mystical sixth sense reveals all. If he likes you, he'll want to know all about you and how you can be employed most profitably. If he doesn't like you, nothing you do will change his obstinate unforgiving mind. If you are not on Scorpio's team, you are a nobody and it's best to make a quick exit. Remember: He is as much a destroyer as he is a builder.

A true charismatic leader to those devoted to him, he can also be competitive, dictatorial, and self-motivating. You can expect to find Scorpio running the most exciting of the *Fortune 500* companies on the new high-tech ventures on the verge of major breakthroughs. Glamour, drama, and power are a part of any Scorpio business as he lands himself and the company on the front page of all the important publications.

Scorpio knows how to rule profitably at the top as no one else does and he is the perfect definition of capitalist boss. However, as genuinely brilliant as he is at managing and controlling the ship of state, beware of those times his intense energy and unbridled passion overwhelm his cool calculated intelligence. Scorpio decisions made in the heat of his emotions are extremely destructive.

Scorpio Success Potential Profile

There is no holding Scorpio back from success (unless his own passion destroys him in the process). An invincible force to reckon with, Scorpio knows who he is and what he can do, and he'll manage to top all the competition so easily that it will look as if his destiny is guided by fate. Intensely ambitious, he reaches the top through his awesome desire for personal wealth and power. Scorpio is a true capitalist with a natural, in-born affinity for making money.

He loves power and he won't stop until he has it all, until he's number one, and nothing can stop him from attaining it. Scorpio relishes crisis and is a master at solving the toughest, most complex problems. Nobody knows the rules of becoming successful better than Scorpio, and he's willing to pay any price for power and wealth. Naturally, Scorpio is capable of abusing power and he must be on guard when his intense, passionate moments begin to rule his senses.

Finally, expect Scorpio to find success in several careers throughout his life. Content to search and seek new challenges, he may walk away from his great success and start again from the ground up. And guess what? He usually makes it to the top again.

ZODIAC MANAGER'S SCORPIO STRATEGY

- Avoid the eyes! Scorpio is the great intimidator and he will try anything to throw you off center and make you feel inferior. This power is reflective in the intensity of his glare and in the slight smirk around the mouth. This physical intimidation is added to his silence, as if anything you say may seem second-rate and unworthy. Don't jump into a conversation because you find the silence is awkward. In other words, upon encountering Scorpio, take your time, relax, don't feel threatened, and refuse to be any less than supremely confident.

- Force Scorpio to face the fact that his intuitive psychic powers may be wrong. Once he begins to question his verdicts, or doubt his hypnotic power over you, the playing field starts to level out.

- Ask questions whenever possible. Find out what Scorpio is thinking or feeling. Knowing what's on his mind or in his heart gives you a little more control over the relationship. Know when to stop so as not to make a formidable enemy, but questions have a way of getting answers and solutions that declarative statements don't. Get him to reveal more of himself than you reveal of you.

- Gain Scorpio's respect, not by winning but by being an equal. The more you can be like him—those moments you are with him—the more he will admire you (as he admires himself).

- Be patient. Let Scorpio play the mind games he loves to play. Don't try to push him into making a decision before he is ready. Intellectual foreplay is his foremost hobby, so let it play itself out. You'll learn what Scorpio is thinking when he is ready to tell you—and not before.

- Exercise polite respect. If Scorpio believes you are trying to undermine his power, he will attack you and attempt to reduce you to the lowest level of worthiness. Don't be slavish, don't be a sycophant, and don't be a flatterer, but do respect him for the good, formidable qualities he possesses.

- Treat Scorpio as somebody. Use fine meals, upscale traveling, classical trapping of power in the office—anything that will say, "This person is important."

- When Scorpio's strength is at its peak, move away. There will be moments when encountering him can only spell disaster. In fact, staying away for healthy periods of time can only serve to add to your strength. Scorpio resents familiarity, so exercise caution and pick your times to be around him judiciously.

- Your main objective must be to create the ideal conditions in which Scorpio can maximize his potential. When operating at full strength, no one can stop him. But his full strength can be sapped if he is faced with mediocre and petty obstacles. Distance him from those tangential issues, decisions, and people who can disrupt his workaholic powers of concentration.

- Check in periodically. What does Scorpio need? What can you do to make it even better?

Scorpio Most Profitable Positions

Actor	FBI Agent	Physician
Advertising Executive	Fireman	Police Officer
Airplane Pilot	Head Hunter	(Detective/Security)
Architect	Historian	Politician
Athlete	Inventor	Producer/Director
Bank Officer	Investment Manager	Producer (Planning)
Chef	Lawyer	Psychiatrist
Chemist	Life Scientist	Psychic
Chief Executive Officer	Manager (Planning;	Purchasing Agent
CIA Officer	Organization)	Radio/TV Personality
Collector	Management	Researcher
Construction Industry	Consultant	Scientist
Employee	Market Analyst	Soldier
Controller	Marketer	Sports Official
Creative Idea Man	Museum Curator	Statistician/
Criminologist	Navigator	Mathematician
Engineer	Newspaper Reporter	Stockbroker
Entertainer	Office Business	Teacher
Entrepreneur	Manager	Technician
Explorer	Physicist	World Leader

Scorpio Most Profitable Location

As with money, we are also dealing with two kinds of Scorpios when it comes to the office. One Scorpio will settle for only the best and most impressive office in the building. He will expect you to spend lavishly to highlight his authority and dominance. And one won't share this throne room with anyone else—although he will be surrounded outside the door by all of his henchman. This Scorpio prefers working alone at the top, in the finest building, in the greatest city in the world. His work location must impress everyone with his unrivalled power, or Scorpio cannot perform to his greatest heights.

The other Scorpio will use his office as a quiet escape from the demands of business. This is his private retreat where he can work out all the problems he is facing and sort through all the complexities to reach the only decision that can be made.

Scorpio Job Skills Rating
1 (Poor) to 5 (Excellent)

Skill	Rating	Skill	Rating
Communications	3	Interpersonal Skills, Teamwork	1
Learning and Thinking Skills	5	Punctuality, Efficiency	4
Work Attitude	5	Loyalty	3
Creativity	3	Technology Skills	4
Problem-Solving	4	Self-Confidence	5
Decision-Making	5	Enthusiasm, Motivation	5
Money Management	4	Self-Management, Initiative	5
Flexibility	3	Honesty, Integrity	3
Accountability, Responsibility	5	Visionary	3
Planning Skills	4	Leadership	5
Details	4		

MANAGING SCORPIO WORKING RELATIONSHIPS

In General

This is a very difficult individual to get close to: He can be bitter, cutting, rude, and unconcerned with other's sensitivities. He can be reserved, aloof, distant, and cool. He is cryptic, revealing little of himself. He dislikes the superficial, powerless, and unintellectual. He is suspicious of others and absolutely unforgiving. He doesn't respond to emotionalism or sentimentality. He is an elitist who seeks only profitable productive friendships. He expects total devotion from true believers. And although he finds it difficult to get involved in a relationship (few are enough for him), once involved, he can become possessive and jealous, and his intense sexual energy can become domineering.

Yet despite all these negatives, there are those who will follow him to the ends of the Earth because of his strictly one-of-a-kind, magnetic aura of power, success, and strength. And once inside the inner circle, these privileged friends will find that no one will be more generous, more concerned, more loyal, and more caring. For these precious deserving few he will go to the ends of the earth.

Summary

Scorpio Working Relationships		
PROFITABLE	RISKY	NON-PROFITABLE
Gemini Virgo	**Taurus** **Sagittarius**	Scorpio Aries Cancer Leo Libra Capricorn Aquarius Pisces

Bottom Line

Scorpio with Scorpio

Put these two together and you have World War III. No bigger battle could ever be waged than one with these two in the ring. This would be a fight to the finish with no winner; the destruction would be total. These are fierce enemies not colleagues.

Scorpio with Sagittarius

Never underestimate Scorpio. In his natural state, the independent Sagittarius will dislike intensely the power hungry Scorpio. However, Scorpio is so clever he may figure out a way to get Sagittarius to do what he wants (make big money) without Sagittarius knowing he's under someone else's thumb. Scorpio's manipulative talent is the key to this duo's productivity. Big money can be made here as long as Sagittarius never feels he is being worked by remote control.

Scorpio with Capricorn

These two signs are enemies. Each is after control and power. Both are calculating and manipulative.

Scorpio with Aquarius

There is nothing the Scorpio boss would love more than to tame his Aquarius employee and control his otherwise frantic exploration. Aquarius, of course, refuses any trap restricting his freedom and is strong and sure enough of himself to fight off the possessive Scorpio and keep his freedom. Scorpio would never have the satisfaction of owning Aquarius, and that's part of his reason for existing: controlling everyone and everything around him. Aquarius is wise enough to keep his independence and avoid slavery.

Scorpio with Pisces

The sensitive, emotionally vulnerable Pisces would be wise to stay clear of this demanding possessive Scorpio boss. Scorpio will see profit potential in creative Pisces, but Pisces should see only trouble. Pisces needs a sympathetic caring boss, not the driven, egocentric dynamo. Scorpio will never understand the freedom or the unstructured environment Pisces needs if he is to become productive. For Scorpio, everyone does it his way or not at all. Pisces should stay away from this duo if he wants to avoid serious emotional injury.

Scorpio with Aries

Stay away from pairing this duo! This is real head-to-head competition. Each is too egocentric and power-hungry to work side-by-side. Both are out to be number one, and no compromise is likely.

Scorpio with Taurus

There is an outside possibility that the financial wizard side of Taurus will work to, for, or, with Scorpio. And there is an excellent chance Scorpio will want Taurus to manage his financial empire. But these are two demanding egos and sparks are bound to fly sooner or later. Nevertheless, if they can make it work, this is a mega-profit duo.

Scorpio with Gemini

Scorpio is the ideal boss for the brilliant, but erratic, Gemini. Scorpio's single-minded drive for power will help his Gemini employee focus his talents in a most profitable direction. It won't be easy for Gemini to work under the dictatorial and demanding Scorpio, but there is big money to be made from this pairing if they can keep their emotions under control. There is big-league productivity here.

Scorpio with Cancer

No question, Cancer profits from strong management, but a Scorpio as head of management would be lethal. Scorpio has no time for Cancer's pace and lack of competitiveness. Scorpio demands prompt productivity and Cancer simply cannot work that efficiently. Obviously, Cancer should never attempt to manage Scorpio (he would lack the strength), nor would he find it worthwhile as a coworker.

Scorpio with Leo

These are two competitors both looking for power. This pairing would be fiercely contested, leaving behind a great deal of destruction before it was all over. Each is after the number-one decision-making role and you don't need two of these types around the office. Don't expect Leo to work for Scorpio or Scorpio for Leo.

Scorpio with Virgo

This is a capitalistic love match. These are two extraordinarily competent and profitable workaholics and you can expect precision and efficiency when they are paired—with Scorpio as boss of course. This is the kind of manager Virgo has been looking for: a manager Virgo can respect and who is as conscientious as he is about every facet of the business. Scorpio, likewise, will find in Virgo his competent reliable alter ego. This may be the most productive duo in the zodiac.

Scorpio with Libra

Scorpio is capitalism defined. Libra needs careful coaxing to even become involved in the capitalist race. Scorpio will simply have no time for someone he considers as commercially out of step as Libra. Libra offers the efficient, productive, and driven Scorpio nothing at all in a business relationship.

ASTRAL FAX #8:
CUSTOMER HOT BUTTONS

The customer is a puzzle! What does he really want? How do you sell him? What is he looking for? What are his "hot buttons?" The *Zodiac Manager* will look first at his customers's sun sign to understand the most important person to him or his business.

Aries: A tough sell. Wants to show you how brilliant he is. Sell him by making him realize how smart he will look buying your product/service. Let him feel like the winner in the deal.

Taurus: A number-cruncher, you need to sell Taurus on price, cost, efficiency, durability, and the investment nature of the product/service.

Gemini: Will want to know everything there is to know about what he is buying. Send the smartest, most knowledgeable, and most experienced person you have.

Cancer: Price is important, but most important is that he wants to buy from a friend. Relationship selling is vital here.

Leo: Sell the "toy" in your product/service. Leo loves to play, and the more toys in his sandbox the better. A theatrical sell is even better.

Virgo: A practical buyer, approach this customer with the facts and nothing but the facts. With Virgo, truth is better than fiction.

Libra: Expect to take on the pros and cons and expect a lengthy decision-making process. Playing Libra's partner in the transaction can speed things up, however.

Scorpio: Scorpio must sell himself. Let him fully explore your offering on his own. All you can do is present your case as if you were presenting it to the king.

Sagittarius: Send a real pro to match wits with this intellectual buyer. He will be all over the place, and not just focusing on your product/service. Expect to play games.

Capricorn: Sell this practical sign on value for money. This is a professional who cares much more about utility than show.

Aquarius: The analytical, enquiring Aquarius buys for his reasons, not yours. Too independent to sell, but always be available to answer questions and offer support for your product/service.

Pisces: Send a "real" salesperson. Pisces has difficulty deciding, so you will need a compassionate, caring persuader to help this sun sign feel comfortable with the purchase.

IX

Managing Sagittarius

November 23–December 21
Symbol: The Archer
Planet: Jupiter
Element: Fire
Motto: "I am I, Don Quixote"

A HISTORIC SAMPLING OF THE SAGITTARIUS WORKFORCE

Woody Allen	Joan Armatrading
Larry Bird	Emily Dickinson
Winston Churchill	Jane Fonda
Joe DiMaggio	Betty Grable
Walt Disney	Florence Griffith Joyner
Jimi Hendrix	Caroline Kennedy
Scott Joplin	Mary Martin
Harpo Marx	Cathy Rigby
Richard Pryor	Diane Sawyer
Charles Schulz	Tina Turner
Mark Twain	Dionne Warwick

A CONFIDENTIAL LISTING OF YOUR SAGITTARIUS
MANAGERS, EMPLOYEES, AND COLLEAGUES

Name	Birth Date	Position

INTRODUCING SAGITTARIUS

A Water sign, Sagittarius is ruled by Jupiter, the largest planet in the solar system. Being as expansive as its ruling planet is what is most attractive about Sagittarius. A lively, independent spirit, this sun sign optimistically explores life in an effort to reach for the stars. "Think big, inspire others, and have fun" is the guiding motto.

This is the eternal student and traveler who cannot stay in any one place for very long. With great energy and enthusiasm she searches for knowledge and to discover unknown lands. There is also a touch of idealism possessed by this joyful communicator as she entertains others with her adventures.

Charisma and excitement drive others to circle this very popular sun sign. And her discoveries can take them to brave new worlds.

Sagittarius Energy Profile

Motion! Physical and mental motion! In fact, it's been said that for the Sagittarian that she is forever in an airport departure as if preparing for the next adventure. Frequent flyer miles were tailor-made for this million-mile traveler. This is an aggressive thoroughbred constantly moving, constantly in search of new experiences and new ideas. This is an enthusiastic, restless traveler requiring a lot of open space to run in, a tireless pursuer of new horizons and wisdom, capable of scattering her energy unproductively and taking on many projects at once. Sagittarius is often unable to concentrate her energy in one purposeful direction. Impatient and quick to move, she is also drawn to dangerous situations. This seems to be her calling—all her life she will be recklessly hunting and searching for the very new, and she'll have a terrific time doing it for life is never stationary, it is a quest.

Sagittarius Personality Profile

Known as the comedian of the zodiac, no doubt voted "most popular" in school, this may be one of the most unforgettable characters you've ever met. All right, so occasionally she exaggerates or can be tactless, blunt, and irresponsible, but that's her enthusiasm working overtime. This sun sign gets real pleasure out of life. She's the clown with the clever wit and an appealing smile. She's the external optimist, convinced that it will all work out for the better. Sagittarians live for the moment (forget the past) and rarely do you find them down on themselves or on others. This is an optimistic thinker ("no " is not in her vocabulary) who believes everything is beautiful and everyone is a friend. That makes her refreshingly cheerful, an adventurous spirit, and one of life's most fascinating and unforgettable characters—a rugged individualist with an unconventional, spontaneous lifestyle who, like Frank Sinatra, will "do it my way."

Sagittarius is also the Peter Pan of the zodiac, a free spirit and a child for life who never tires of performing in a three-ring circus of her own design.

Generous to a fault and a born philanthropist for those in true need, she is also a fighter with a strong code of ideals and ethics, a defender of the underdog, and a staunch believer in justice, fairness, and honesty. Sensitive to social issues, you will frequently find her fighting for a cause, seeking to create the best of all possible worlds.

Courageous and fearless, Sagittarius will try just about anything, and this compulsive, erratic behavior is often mistaken for irresponsibility. Playing the role of a modern Marco Polo, Sagittarius can be delightful, but a maddeningly careless individual. This is a real performer who loves applause and is easily hurt when she doesn't get it. But she is amazingly resilient, and her wounds heal very quickly. So when she does become unglued or angry it's serious and it will happen suddenly, then it will immediately disappear.

Eccentric, unpredictable, and chaotic—everyone enjoys watching the adventurous Sagittarius perform, including herself. A real role player, she likes to play the swashbuckling hero and any other role that can win her center-ring attention. (Sagittarians are unquestionably narcissistic). Another role she takes very seriously is the role of professor. Underneath these theatrics is an individual with a serious scholarly investment in psychiatry/philosophy/religion, in particular. And although the tendency is to simply enjoy being Sagittarius, the fact is, she secretly offers an intelligence, creativity, and curiosity far beyond most signs you'll meet.

Outwardly fun and enthusiastic, Sagittarius retains her youthful outlook on life. For her, the future is what is important and all she requires is the freedom to pursue it anyway she desires. If Sagittarius is anything, she is a free woman. This one will never be fenced in. (This is also true of relationships as well as in her professional life.) Sagittarius cannot accept possessiveness, and it takes a very special partner/family/company to understand this.

Sagittarius needs land and exercise (physical and mental). She is a versatile and talented performer and can be found in a wide range of activities.

And the bottom line is, it's a real pleasure to know and to be a Sagittarian. They can be simply terrific! Oh, yes—and lucky, very lucky.

Sagittarius Intelligence Profile

The stand-up comic! Sagittarius is the philosopher, pedant, eternal student, and teacher who is in pursuit of the ultimate truth and the ultimate good. Sagittarius leads a life in continuous search of knowledge and wisdom and there is no limitation on how far her search can take her. This is a highly intelligent, interdisciplinary scholar with an impressive breadth of vision and a very clever wit to accompany it. Totally confident Sagittarius has a quick mind with excellent powers of observation and a curiosity about the future that is virtually unrivaled. Industrious and studious, there isn't anything she doesn't find interesting. With extraordinary motivation she explores the unknown with great ingenuity in search of new solutions. The Sagittarius imagination, which is vivid, is frequently put to practical use, as is her great intuition. As active mentally as she is physically, Sagittarius can also suffer from understanding too quickly and not thinking things all the way through. Anyone who moves through fields of knowledge (as well as life) as quickly as she does is bound to overlook some critical details and jump to some wrong conclusions. She also has a tendency to scrap one area of knowledge for another before she's done all the work. But she's wise enough to realize, eventually, when she's wrong, and she really does learn from her mistakes.

Sagittarius Communications Profile

On those infrequent occasions when Sagittarius is not on the move, physically, you're likely to find her tongue on the move. The word *gregarious* was invented for Sagittarius. This is a talker! However, she may be talking so rapidly that she doesn't make sense. This is a very smart, funny person, but many times she does herself an injustice by responding so quickly that her remarks sound glib and shallow, rather than considerate.

Although a boisterous, funny, and friendly questioner and persuader, this sun sign is not known primarily as a verbal communicator (although her stories are fascinating). Sagittarians communicate through deeds and action. They are, however, legendary for clearly verbalizing one thing: the absolute unadulterated truth! Ask Sagittarius her opinion and her answer will be blunt and totally honest ("I cannot tell a lie."), yet free of harmless intent. "Harm" she relegates to her argumentative debating side where her coolly reserved arguments, laced with satire and wit, surgically cut through any opposition.

Sagittarius's restlessness makes it difficult to carry on a complete conversation with her and that's a shame. She has an ingenious mind and has lived the kind of adventurous life anyone would want to hear about.

Sagittarius Diplomacy Profile

She probably thinks she would make a terrific diplomat. She's charismatic and a joy to be with, and she tells a great tale; but she's too damned honest and independent-minded. It is simply unnatural for a Sagittarius to tell a lie or to be deceitful. In diplomatic circles, her honesty would be considered tactless. Naturally, Sagittarius would love to be in the diplomatic spotlight but her total disregard for diplomacy and duplicity make her more an instrument of war than an instrument of peace.

Sagittarius Money Profile

Talk about the last of the big time spenders! All she does is spend. In fact, she'll buy things she doesn't even need. She's impulsive. She's generous (making her friends very happy) and will pick up the tab every time. She's a gambler who'll bet on anything regardless of the odds. (She can win big or lose big, but nothing in-between.)

And despite all this spending, she is usually able to make all the money she'll ever need. This is both "millionaire and bankruptcy country." Wealth is security to Sagittarius (it pays for her freedom and her unconventional lifestyle), so one of her priorities is to make all she can get. But she doesn't count it and probably wouldn't even mind it if she occasionally goes broke (temporarily, of course). She's resilient enough to make it back. Money is also part of Sagittarius's theatrics. Wealth allows her to put on any kind of show she wants and allows her to experience any adventure she wants, as well as supporting her extensive travels.

Sagittarius will not be won over with tales of future earnings, pleas, or stock options. She wants it now because plans for her next adventure are already on her mind.

Sagittarius Loyalty Profile

Sagittarius is extremely loyal to herself, to freedom, to wisdom, and to adventure. Certainly her buddies are loyal to her—she is a terrifically generous, jovial, and entertaining person. However, Sagittarius considers loyalty to others as restraining and inhibiting. Change is part of life, believes Sagittarius, and friendships must change as well as everything else. Also, Sagittarius's constant movement can put her out of touch for long periods. Of course she needs friends because she loves applause and loves company (her friends come from all walks of life) but she is not particularly loyal to them in the traditional sense. She doesn't know them well enough, for one thing, and for another, her loyalty to herself and her desires are much more important.

Sagittarius Work Habits Profile

Expect the unusual, and give her space. A claustrophobic environment is the least productive place for a Sagittarius. She needs freedom—no schedules, no routine, no nine to five. She must be allowed to experience her mind and to keep actively exploring. This is a jack-of-all-trades who can become totally bored without a versatile, multijob position, which allows for travel and discovery.

This is also an employee with a superiority complex, and she's not afraid of telling anyone, even the boss, that he or she is dead wrong. Honesty and bluntness are her strong suit. Yet she is extremely likable, popular, and a superior company frontwoman, even though her decidedly truthful comments may be tactless at times.

Sagittarius is smart and versatile enough to do anything you need her to do, but try to ask for her help, not demand it. She needs to feel that she is managing her own life and has been given great latitude to handle the job as she sees fit. Once committed (even though it is a temporary commitment), she's responsible and dependable; she goes after the greatest challenges with undeniable energy, and she is so quick at uncovering ingenious solutions that she should be given control of several assignments at once to keep her interested. Pressure and deadline are what she thrives on. However, because of her fast pace and many interests, she doesn't always finish what she started. This is a "big picture" employee who doesn't pay enough attention to detail and who can start talking recklessly before she starts thinking.

Highly competitive, Sagittarius is an original: an individualist who is spontaneous and changeable, yet possessing superb business skills. She is a solution-oriented decision-maker, an expert persuader, promoter, and negotiator. She is a friendly, witty employee with a lot of friends (despite her occasional impatience). A risk-taking but productive worker, she's a commercially creative businesswoman and a quality manipulator. However, only the less structured, more loosely organized business suits her best—a business that has flexible responsibilities, multiple products, and a freedom orientation will suit her active curious spirit and her broad range of interest. Sagittarius will take on the company's most adventurous job (preferably, going it alone), and she will expect megabucks in return (and she will usually deserve them). "It takes money to make money" is her byword.

A speedy worker, she dismisses the direction of others because she is frequently farther ahead of their orders. But this is not to say Sagittarius doesn't need direction. In fact, she needs a lot of well-reasoned direction from the person who has earned her respect.

The Sagittarian can also be unreliable, irresponsible, disorganized, and late. She can promise the Earth, stars, and moon but then get sidetracked on a more challenging jaunt. She can lack discipline and direction. She is capable of pontificating like the best barroom philosopher or revolutionary without taking up the sword and marching into battle. (As they say in Texas, "all hat and no cattle.") Her chaotic style can diminish her achievements, and her anti-career track attitude can reduce her level of experience. But respect and well-reasoned management can help Sagittarius stay focused enough on the goal to achieve great things—obviously a full-time job for any boss.

This is not your average employee. This is a gambler, a speculator. She's the one leading you into the next decade in her unique, independent, and unbending manner. If your company can't fit an individualistic dynamo like this into the organizational chart, forget it. The fit between her and the position must be letter perfect to work for both of you. And if you can make the fit, don't forget that hands-off, subtle management is the only kind of management that a loner such as Sagittarius will allow.

Sagittarius Leadership Profile

Sagittarius does it with style, glamour, and extravagance. In her very lively "offices"—wherever they may be—her employees will delight in her enthusiastic, generous, fair, and expansive managerial manner. But she will be blunt and honest. She will expect work done quickly and will be tough on those who don't deliver. She will also expect total loyalty and dedication.

Sagittarius is a natural born executive of the never-in-the-office-always-in-the-field school. She's out overseeing the big picture (her employees are handling the details) or creating vast futuristic projects, and when she's finished with it, she's off to another project, leaving an inspired band of workers to finish up.

This is an exploring risk-taking boss. She's an intelligent gambler betting on the future, and her company must be as versatile and as flexible as she is to handle such a vast array of challenges.

Sagittarius leaders play fastball. Things happen quickly and on a large scale. She'll win more of these games of educated chance than she'll lose, but at times it will be unnerving, undisciplined, hectic, and downright lucky. And she is precisely why many Sagittarius leaders perform independently, alone, or over only the most lenient enterprise. Sagittarius must be "the boss" because other "boss" signs rarely allow such high-risk behavior. A genuine entrepreneur, she does it her unorthodox way or not at all. And it's never dull.

Sagittarius Success Potential Profile

So doing well above the trivial, Sagittarius aims at going all the way, getting all she can out of life, forever seeking new frontiers to explore. Success comes her way with seemingly little effort. She thrives on the hope of directing a large-scale, creative enterprise with a free hand. She loves the challenge of moving from adventure to adventure, accumulating fascinating personal experiences and extensive knowledge. Her resilience allows her to overcome barrier after barrier. She's serious about making a lot of money so that she never loses her freedom. She craves learning. She loves the spotlight, the applause, the life of a star. She's lucky, brilliant, and quick. She's a promoter. And she'll do anything for a laugh.

Luckier than any other zodiac sign, this highly motivated, self-assured, individualist is an enthusiastic winner who seems to make it big her way without excessive strain and without following the rules of the corporate game. Not only does she look and act like a success, but she usually is one in the frantic world of the gambler.

ZODIAC MANAGER'S SAGITTARIUS STRATEGY

- Be prepared to be insulted—in fun, but insulted nonetheless. Sagittarius finds it hard to be serious, and even a legitimately serious question is likely to draw a humorous response. Don't take offense. Sagittarius can't help herself and she can't turn off her devilishly comedic mind. She'll give you a respectful answer soon enough so let her finish her performance first. She'll feel better for it and the serious answer will certainly be worth waiting for.

- Be prepared to coach. Sagittarius is a diamond in the rough when it comes to business, and you will need to carve a business mind out of this outstanding, but raw, material. Still it won't be easy, because Sagittarius believes she knows more than you do, even though she may have just joined the firm and you've been with it for decades. The moment she signs on, Sagittarius's mind will be racing ahead with ideas, solutions, plans, and visions. It will be up to you to teach Sagittarius to continue to soar, but in formation. She needs to be coached in discipline, budgeting of time and money, responsibility and accountability, scheduling, working with others, respect for company executives, and corporate culture—in short, a mini-MBA course. And you'll need all the patience and perseverance at your command to coach her. Match her wit, trump her sense of reason, show off your own creativity, and develop a respectful relationship—these are guidelines to be adhered to in order to get Sagittarius's attention and to get her to learn.

- Give Sagittarius time to perform alone in the spotlight. Give her an assignment that stretches her mind and her sense of adventure. Give her something for her alone to explore. Few signs in the zodiac will surprise you with creative results as this one. This will also win her over to you and the company because you have given her the space she needs to expand her world. Keep in mind that this assignment is as important to her as anything else she's doing for the company, so give time to hear her reports and record and highlight her achievements.

- Prevent Sagittarius's boredom by setting in front of her a plate of multi-jobs—not so many that they will only "improve" her lack of discipline, but enough that will make each day a little different. Her flexible mind needs variety to stay sharp. It needs to be constantly challenged. A variety of associated assignments will do wonders to motivate her and help her grow quickly.

- Provide the opportunity for Sagittarius to become involved in social causes supported by the company. There is a strong nurturing and philanthropic side to Sagittarius, and being allowed to exhibit it under the corporate umbrella will increase her loyalty. Likewise, provide Sagittarius with an opportunity to teach. Sharing her experiences, adventures, and philosophy is important to her, a gift she genuinely enjoys giving others, inspiring them to undertake adventures of their own.

- Give her a suitcase, a world map, a handful of tickets, and let her go. Desk jobs debilitate. The airways invigorate. Fieldwork, onsite surveys, and foreign opportunities—these are all areas in which this world class traveler can shine.

- She will discover more opportunities for you from her traveling than even she would uncover with all her creativity at corporate headquarters.

- Wanted: world-class support staff. To pick up the pieces, to follow through, to get Sagittarius there on time, to do the detail work, to keep in constant touch with her wherever she is in the world, you will need the worker bees. Thank God for cellular phones, but be prepared to replace her lost ones frequently. With all Sagittarius's constant mental and physical motion, a safety net must be in place everywhere she goes. And only your best, quick-thinking "aides" need apply for this job.

- Sagittarius craves visibility. Give her plenty of press. It will make her feel appreciated. The more applause the better. But also be prepared to take an occasional intermission from Sagittarius's performance. Take time to download Sagittarius's achievements and adventures and to learn all about what she's been up to so that nothing is lost along the way. This must be a thorough debriefing, because Sagittarius is certain to run through her experience as quick as she can.

- Change is Sagittarius's mantra. So her loyalty must be of great concern to you. Her need to expand and discover, both personally and professionally, must be recognized and encouraged. It will keep her loyal to you and it will keep her as fresh and as brilliant as she desires to be. It's a win-win for both of you.

Sagittarius Most Profitable Positions

Actor	Explorer	Newspaper Reporter
Advertising Executive	Farmer	Oceanographer
Athlete/Sportswriter	Guru	Philanthropist
Book Seller	Head Hunter	Philosopher
Cartoonist	Horse Trainer	Politician
Clergyman	Import/Export	Photographer
Collector	Employee	Producer/Director
Comedian/Comic	Interpreter	Public Relations
Writer	Inventor	Executive
Creative Director	Librarian	Radio/TV Personality
Creative Idea	Life Scientist	Retailer
Person	Management	Salesperson
Diplomat	Consultant	Self-Employed
Dog Breeder	Marketing Manager	Sportsman
Editor/Publisher	Merchandising	Teacher
Entertainer	Employee	Transportation
Entrepreneur	New Product Developer	Travel Agent
		Veterinarian

Sagittarius Most Profitable Location

There is no one location for Sagittarius. A nomad, this sun sign is everywhere satisfying her inquiring mind. Sagittarius is a perpetual motion machine pursuing high-risk adventure, and no office is ever going to hold her. However, as she performs her fieldwork she will spend big money on her temporary workspace, a wide-open space with high ceilings, large window plants, and travel posters.

Sagittarius Job Skills Rating			
1 (Poor) to 5 (Excellent)			
Communications	4	Interpersonal Skills, Teamwork	4
Learning and Thinking Skills	4	Punctuality, Efficiency	2
Work Attitude	3	Loyalty	4
Creativity	4	Technology Skills	3
Problem-Solving	4	Self-Confidence	5
Decision-Making	3	Enthusiasm, Motivation	4
Money Management	2	Self-Management, Initiative	3
Flexibility	5	Honesty, Integrity	3
Accountability, Responsibility	3	Visionary	4
Planning Skills	2	Leadership	4
Details	2		

MANAGING SAGITTARIUS WORKING RELATIONSHIPS

In General

Has she got friends! Like a magnet, they are automatically drawn to her without any effort on her part. You could fill the Rose Bowl with them. But if you look closely, most of them are really admiring fans more than close friends. Sagittarius is simply on the move too much to form close relationships.

Nevertheless, Sagittarius enjoys the attention of her fans who come from every walk of life and form a very loyal group. This is the original "Hail-Fellow, Well Met" (and sometimes "Glad Hand"), who is always there with a story and a drink and the makings of a party. Sagittarius is a great host, great guest, and entertainer, and she'll make you feel like a friend even though you'll never become a close one.

She will, however, find time for several close intimates (women and men), because it takes more than one to satisfy her physically and mentally. To these, she is devoted and demanding in her unique way. Yet although she loves only a few, many love her.

Summary

Sagittarius Working Relationships		
PROFITABLE	RISKY	NON-PROFITABLE
Capricorn	Sagittarius Taurus Gemini Leo Virgo Scorpio Aquarius	Aries Cancer Libra Pisces

Bottom Line

Sagittarius with Sagittarius

These two will have a terrific time together, the short time they are together. Everyone will find them a total delight and exciting to watch and listen to. But their individualism and their pace will keep them apart most of the time. Socially, everyone will profit from the pairing. Commercially, they are too independent to work side by side, except in a loose partnership that allows great freedom for each of them. Then these two could be very productive.

Sagittarius with Capricorn

If only they could get together. The adventurous, far-flung Sagittarius makes things happen in a dozen different ways. Capricorn can take all those things, put them together, and make them profitable. Sagittarius explores and creates, Capricorn plans and manages. This could mean big money. The problem is the battle will be between Sagittarius's freedom vs. Capricorn's control. However, the capitalistic Capricorn will probably be smart enough to realize that because Sagittarius's freedom brings in the dollars, enlightened management is called for. As long as Capricorn can appear to keep her hands off and as long as the money comes in the opportunistic Capricorn will hang on to this delicate relationship.

Sagittarius with Aquarius

There are very similar, freedom-loving, investigative personalities here. But their love for freedom and their independent self-confidence will make it very difficult for them to work together. They certainly will enjoy sharing ideas and experiences one with the other, but together, day to day, can stifle their experimentation. This can be a highly profitable duo if they are only loosely associated and come together only on selected occasions to present the results of their latest adventures, and it won't be easy to keep them in a room long enough to make it all productive.

Sagittarius with Pisces

Here are two friendly, creative characters who will enjoy one another's stories and company. However, there is very little to be gained from a commercial company. Sagittarius prefers her independence and her multi-directional lifestyle. She is not interested in being the enlightened manager to a sensitive, imaginative, and vulnerable dreamer. Sagittarius is a non-stop doer, and she simply doesn't have time to slow down for the fragile Pisces.

Sagittarius with Aries

These are two very strong, very independent personalities. It is difficult to imagine anything profitable coming out of such a pairing simply because such superiority complexes would be unable to yield or to share or work together on anything. Both are "stars" seeking the spotlight. Antagonism and competition result here, not cooperation. Given the intense energy level of each, they wouldn't have time to sit down and work anything out anyway.

Sagittarius with Taurus

They are total opposites: slow and conservative vs. motion and risk. On the one hand, this gives the pair great balance, complimenting each other's skills. But they are so different, they may be only able to suffer each other a short period of time. This could be a very profitable duo if Taurus is patient with the expensive, adventurous, exploring Sagittarius. But she will expect Sagittarius to deliver big bucks in exchange for the freedom. It's very chancy, but it's certainly worth trying.

Sagittarius with Gemini

This is a pairing of two of the most spontaneous individuals in the zodiac. The results of their efforts will be fascinating. Unfortunately, you may never see the combined results because they may choose not to work together (loners), or they may simply decide to go off in another direction. The most sophisticated management skills will be necessary here to produce profits. It can be done, but these brilliant, unconventional characters are very difficult to guide together along the same path.

Sagittarius with Cancer

Sagittarius is the kind of romantic hero that Cancer can worship. But in the cold commercial world this relationship will produce little of value. Cautious Cancer simply cannot keep pace with the enthusiastic and adventurous Sagittarius. They're two creative personalities, yes, but they operate on different levels of the stratosphere. Except for appreciating her applause, Sagittarius won't even know Cancer is around.

Sagittarius with Leo

If you can get them to work together in an informal partnership, you should do it. These two are capable of brilliant results. But these independent showboating personalities won't be easy to keep on target. And what could be worse, Leo might try to take command. Big dollars are possible here in risky ventures. Stability and consistency are the problems.

Sagittarius with Virgo

A Virgo employee can make Sagittarius efficient and productive. Virgo's administrative skills and attention to detail are exactly what the globetrotting Sagittarius needs. However, if Virgo's demands begin to restrict Sagittarius's freedom, it's all over. There is a delicate balance that must be maintained to avoid constant friction.

Sagittarius with Libra

Chances are Libra won't even try to keep with the self-assured, individualistic Sagittarius. Libra will be her greatest fan and a worshiper, but otherwise she offers no commercial value to Sagittarius. Sagittarius simply does not have the time to help what she will consider to be an ineffective personality. Libra needs understanding and guidance, not avoidance.

Sagittarius with Scorpio

Never underestimate Scorpio. In her natural state, the independent Sagittarius will dislike the power-hungry Scorpio intensely. However, Scorpio is so clever that she may figure out a way to get Sagittarius to do what she wants (make big money) without Sagittarius knowing she's under someone else's thumb. How talented Scorpio is at manipulation is the key to this duo's productivity. Big money can be made here as long as Sagittarius never feels she is being worked by remote control.

Astral Fax #9: "Stars" Over Wall Street

According to the ninth Astrology and Stock Market Conference, held in New York on May 17, 2001, investors who think they have tried every strategy under the sun may want to start looking to the stars. Using astrology to guide investment decisions comes as no surprise to Henry Weingarten, founder of the Astrologers Fund Web site *(www.afund.com)*, whose stargazing investors can foretell market movements, mergers, and company performance.

Weingarten's Astrologers Fund manages between $3 and $4 million using astrology as its primary tool. Weingarten, a professional astrologer for more than 30 years, is the author of *Investing By The Stars* and *Wall Street, Next Week*. Even traditional Wall Street professionals concede that Weingarten's methods seem to have validity. "Some peaks and troughs in the market have correlated with lunar eclipses," says Peter Canelo, U.S. strategist at Morgan Stanley Dean Witter.

Weingarten also uses astrological charts to track major events in companies' lives. Each firm's sign is determined by its incorporation date. For example: Disney and GM are Libras; Coke is a Virgo; and IBM is a

Taurus. Reading AT&T's chart—Ma Bell is a Pisces—Weingarten fore-told problems with its bids for TCI on June 24, 2001. The day after it was announced, Neptune converged with Saturn—a portent of disaster.

Weingarten finds that today's environment forces investors to pick and choose, trading more frequently. "It's not buy and hold; its buy, hold, sell," he said. In his 2001 forecast, well before the big April rally, Weingarten noted that "just as many investors may be upset about not selling more Nasdaq stocks last March, next year they are likely to be upset about not having bought more quality Nasdaq stocks this March." The forecast named International Business Machines (IBM) as the top pick on the Dow Jones Industrial Average, and that stock is now up nearly 40 percent since the start of the year. General Motors Corp. (GM) and AT&T Corp. (T) were favored in the first half, with second-half picks Home Depot Inc. (HD) and Microsoft (MSFT). Weingarten believes that the key to succeeding in the 21st century will be knowing that "employing a business astrologer is a necessity, not a luxury. Hiring one can be as important to a business as employing a lawyer or accountant. A businessman who has both the cour-age and independent thinking which allows him/her to hire an astrologer is already on the road to success."

X

Managing Capricorn

December 22–January 20
Symbol: The Goat
Ruling Planet: Saturn
Element: Earth
Motto: "If It Is To Be...It Is Up To Me"

A HISTORIC SAMPLING OF THE CAPRICORN WORKFORCE

Joan Baez	Clara barton
John Denver	Faye Dunaway
Carlton Fisk	George Foreman
Diane Fossey	Ava Gardner
Howard Hughes	Janis Joplin
Martin Luther King	Barbara Mandrell
Ethel Merman	Isaac Newton
Richard Nixon	Dolly Parton
Elvis Presley	Betsy Ross
Helena Rubinstein	Albert Schweitzer
Susan Sontag	Howard Stern
Woodrow Wilson	Henny Youngman

A CONFIDENTIAL LISTING OF YOUR CAPRICORN
MANAGERS, EMPLOYEES, AND COLLEAGUES

Name	Birth Date	Position

INTRODUCING CAPRICORN

An Earth sign (like Taurus), Capricorn is ruled by the planet Saturn, in mythology, the harvester with a sickle (as we reap what we sow). This is a serious, hardworking, and determined sign dedicated to purpose. Capricorns understand that their road to power and control has many challenges and obstacles. This is reflected in Capricorn's symbol, the Goat, which represents his slow, difficult climb from the pasture to the top of the summit.

A conservative who's respectful of past wisdom and loyally devoted to family, Capricorn tends to avoid public show. Yet we cannot fail to see his ambitious drive at work as he accumulates the power he needs to harvest his hard work.

Practical, economical, and persistent, Capricorns are natural business executives, although their lack of charisma can keep them from hero or leadership status.

Capricorn Energy Profile

We are now going to introduce you to a calm, reserved, calculating individual with a slow, steady, and considered energy, efficiently expended. He's nothing showy, but he always gives more than enough to get the job done; he's never idle and always busy. This does not appear to be an overwhelmingly active individual (nor is he a traveler), but never underestimate him. His conservative energy level, nevertheless, produces high-powered results.

Capricorn is quietly deceptive. Power in substantial quantity exists behind this placid, cool façade. But he is simply using his energy wisely, and in the end he will be the one to win the race against his more frantic rivals (he is the tortoise, not the hare). You will never see Capricorn rush into anything, but you will see him quietly persevering, climbing to the top, in carefully measured miles, without ever stopping to take a break.

Capricorn Personality Profile

This is a 100-percent conservative, conventional personality—a traditionalist who believes in family, home, church, business, and patriotism. Solid, dependable, and reliable, Capricorn is the rock on which our nation was founded. You will also find him as impenetrable as rock, tough to know, with a reserved, stuffy, and frequently snobbish presence.

Capricorns need not only a stable society to exist in, but they also need a stable family. (Never rock the Capricorn boat.) At heart he is a father figure (stern but fair) who demands respect and obedience. In return he is loving, giving, and devoted to his family. Curiously, this attachment to family and society is not an emotional one, but a carefully reasoned and logical relationship. In fact, the outward show of emotion is just not in the cool Capricorn's repertoire. Not impulsive, passionate, or jealous, his reactions are invariably mental; however, this strict facade can crack occasionally with a terrific off-the-wall sense of humor that surprises and delights his audience.

This is an individual intent on maintaining an impressive reputation. Deference, demeanor, and propriety are very important to Capricorn and social, as well as financial, prominence is critical. Status-conscious to a fault, virtually everything Capricorn does has a purpose, reinforcing his impeccable, unflappable civic and professional image. The people he associates with have pedigree, his possessions are tasteful, his dress is proper. His children go to the best schools, and he lives in the best neighborhood. In short, it is critical for Capricorn to be important and to have an unassailable reputation. He also needs desperately to be loved and adored by his fans, forever being told how wonderful he is. That's all part of enhancing his public image.

Capricorn has a high regard for dignity, worth, and fair play. He believes in the constitution, his religion, the family, and the law. Rigidly living in the past, this traditionalist is respectful of old money, education, culture, and heritage. He is the cornerstone of our civilization, and he knows it.

Outwardly, he can appear harmless and indifferent. Inside, this is a very tough, competitive, and calculating individual with a massive ego, whose patient and studied progress through this world are driving him to overcome all barriers on his way to worldly success. For Capricorn's goal is nothing short of dominance, in whatever he does. And he usually achieves it by controlling every aspect of his life and creating his own destiny. Focused, disciplined, and entirely self-motivated, he truly believes that he alone is all he needs to succeed. His control over himself and other's is that complex. Fiercely ambitious, he is sole initiator of his vision, and he will sacrifice anything (except perhaps family) to realize that vision by his carefully planned actions.

Even deeper inside, but rarely seen, is the tendency for serious depression. This is a genuine worrier with doubts and fears about who he really is. This is a pessimist for whom victory isn't ever good enough. At the core of this individual is a shy, sensitive, emotional, and lonely person who has given in to the strict demands of his outward personality, an overserious individual prone to melancholy and doubt in his private moments, but required to be above human frailty in his public role. Naturally, this is a secret he doesn't dare let out, but when you see the petulant, uncontrolled, and even depressed side of Capricorn, you now know where it's coming from.

A curiosity: Capricorns get younger as they get older. As a result, success usually comes later in life—when they are young! Capricorns construct a cold brick wall around a delicate core—a facade of great endurance, strength, and determination. Capricorns fight themselves to emerge self-confident and self-assured. Their important friends and possessions must constantly reinforce their personal value and worth. Capricorn is a self-constructed man playing for the biggest commercial stakes life has to offer and playing at a significant personal cost, but he has no choice. The stars have chosen his destiny for him; he must attain dominance and all the world must recognize it.

Capricorn Intelligence Profile

This is an industrious mind with great powers of concentration, which allow it to absorb and learn almost anything. Capricorn is a super-achiever, and he has the kind of smarts that supports advancement. This is a serious, rational, hardworking mind with great common sense that is superb at working out problems for profitable conclusions. Capricorn is a patient, ever-slow learner, but only because he wants to be positive he understands everything before he puts his knowledge to use.

A practical mind (although it certainly appreciates the creative arts) this sun sign has a distinctive factual and mathematical aptitude and an intense interest and need for day-to-day knowledge. It is attracted to detail, for example, for these are the kinds of ingredients he needs to make logical decisions. Capricorn will work for days on a given problem and he won't give up until he's done all the homework needed to render a sensible judgement.

At the same time, this highly rational mind has an intuitive, even psychic, side to it. He is a world-class futurist and visionary who can see trends well before others can, a strange combination—the practical and the psychic.

However, there is a disturbing side to Capricorn's intelligence. Because he considers himself in control of his life, he learns mostly from observation than from others. In fact, he judges people very quickly and if he feels they have little to offer (as he frequently does) he cuts them out of the conversation. Capricorn's intellectual arrogance can be self-defeating, and he can lose a valuable source of information and knowledge by his quick dismissal and judgement of others' abilities.

Add to this Capricorn's highly critical nature and his love of playing devil's advocate, and you can end up with a "world according to (only) Capricorn" scenario.

Capricorn Communications Profile

Capable of being a serious mature conversationalist and a concerned listener, Capricorn treats those he respects with care and attention. This is because manners and a sense of propriety are strong Capricorn traits, as well as his strong desire to learn. He is not attracted to showy, frivolous, or gossipy dialogues, although when he decides to jump up on stage he can be a very clever, cynical comedian.

With those he does not respect, however, or with those he considers beneath him, it is a one-way conversation with Capricorn lecturing on what's right and wrong. Because what Capricorn is doing is undoubtedly more important, not to mention correct, he doesn't need to listen to you.

This attitude, coupled with his respectful and correct conversations with power brokers, can lead to nothing but shallow dialogues, because Capricorn frequently fails to find substantial value in talking with anyone.

Capricorn Diplomacy Profile

An elegant host and guest, Capricorn believes he is unrivaled diplomats and no doubt about it, he is very, very good at it. Capricorn loves associating in this kind of world and demonstrating his considerable social graces, manners, and unimpeachable politics. Capricorn political sensitivities shine in these kinds of settings, and, even though he may not be particularly fond of all the people there, his sense of propriety will win out. This is truly the kind of center stage, role-playing event that the socially conscious Capricorn loves. From the diplomat's view, they may find this individual somewhat reserved, distant, and even snobbish, because of Capricorn's forced yet impressive upper class image. But this sun sign does know how to handle himself. He's learned to be acceptable, he's learned formal social manners and good graces, and, like fine wine, these are staples for diplomatic affairs.

Capricorn Money Profile

Capricorn is very serious about money. He's a serious financial planner and frugal conservative moneyman—no get rich quick schemes here.

This is a prudent individual who carefully calculates earnings and savings so that he will never face financial insecurity. Above all, he is fearful of poverty. His money dealings and arrangements are designed to provide a reliable and comfortable income for life. He is a discriminating shopper (sometimes stingy and miserly) and is an accomplished bargain-hunter and cost-saver. Never wasteful of his cash, he will negotiate to the penny, in his favor, so don't expect big money contracts come easily from him.

Although Capricorn loves to accumulate money, he is also a true materialist and can't resist elegant surroundings and fashionable possessions. Disgusted by showy, flamboyant items, this sun sign spends considerable sums on the very best (and most expensive) that is made only with quiet, sophisticated good taste, purchases, that, in turn, reflect his good taste to his cultured and moneyed acquaintances. In fact, he frequently becomes his possessions so closely do they become a part of him.

This is a big money-maker even though he is a strict, risk-avoiding conservative. Through cautious opportunism this financial wizard builds up his money supply slowly but steadily, and late in life he can emerge as one of businesses biggest moguls.

Capricorn Loyalty Profile

Capricorn is very loyal to his country, religion, company, family, and career. After all, these are the cornerstones of our society, and this strict traditionalist believes in his heritage and in seeing it continued. He is also loyal to our nation and to ethical principles, morality, honesty, and justice.

Capricorn is extremely loyal to his employer, his close business associates, and his business, and he demands loyalty from them in return. When Capricorn makes a commitment, he is serious about it, and you better be, too. Duty and obedience are important to him. Loyalty is a quality you dare not cheat on with Capricorn. If you do, he'll be finished with you forever, no questions asked.

Capricorn Work Habits Profile

This is a sign with a true passion for business. Capricorn is a born businessman. Industrious and committed to a career, he will take on any job you give him and do it supremely well. Thriving on detail, Capricorn will overlook nothing—no cheating and no short cuts. He could care less about the time clock and he'll work overtime as a matter of course because he's a workaholic. Capricorn is highly organized. In fact, his life and career have been carefully planned and he will not be distracted from his programmed career goals. Capricorn thrives on responsibility, and you'll find no one more conscientious, so whenever you can, put him in control—after all, that's his natural role. This sun sign performs best in positions that require street-smart, practical intelligence (drawn from his vast collection of facts) and logical decision-making capabilities.

He is not a fast or impulsive worker, so don't push or change directions on him. He is patient, thorough, careful, and cautious—tolerating no mistakes. His results are virtually flawless. Also, although this by-the-book employee is following the rules, in the process of doing his job by the letter of the law, he is also capable of developing new solutions or different, more profitable applications or approaches.

All these professional work habits are motivated by extreme ambition. All this toiling and hard work, all this concentration of energy is designed to initiate the process and lay the groundwork on which Capricorn intends to build his impressive career. Capricorn plans from day one how he can progress steadily through the company to the top. So, after exercising his skills, while he's in your employment, he will expect you to recognize his talents and reward them. He will expect you to promote him, raise his salary, and praise him. And because he is a very productive worker, and may very well be your boss sometime in the future, while he is with you, treat him very well.

Capricorn works best in a practical, clearly defined job where his logical mind can make the most profitable decisions. Preferring neither to travel nor to be disturbed, an attractive and impressive work area or office solely for him will be most appreciated. A superb employee, as well as a loner with a superiority complex, he is truly capable of doing it all. So while he's working for you, give him everything you can. He can take you far as long as you reward his efforts.

Capricorn Leadership Profile

This is not a born leader, but everything he does in his life makes him one. Everything he does and learns are but stepping stones to a position of total authority and control. Carefully, the Capricorn goals are climbing the mountain, avoiding disaster, bouncing back from defeat, and learning as he goes steadily up to the summit.

Once he reaches that magnificent and tasteful office at the top, he rules alone. He is the authority figure—his managerial skills are excellent and there isn't anything he doesn't know about the enterprise. He has prepared himself for every situation and has run fire drills on how to handle potential disaster. Capricorn plays this star-studded romantic leadership role supremely well—after all, he's been rehearsing all his life; he is definitely in charge, the commander-in-chief. He makes it all happen his way. He is all work and he expects everybody else to be, too. This is the boss, the father of the company, and he runs the business as he runs his own life and home: He will be concerned, just, firm, and sympathetic, but definitely in command. He will expect his business family to be obedient and respectful. He will expect them to be honest and loyal. He'll expect them to be smart and industrious. After all, that's what the old man is (and more).

Although Capricorn appears dignified and reserved, he's street tough and knows how to manipulate deals to get whatever he wants. Workers below standards will be particular targets for dismissal. Financially the company will be profitable but conservative. The corporate style will exude taste and quality and will be highly visible and prominent in the community.

Capricorn leadership is also highly political in nature and many from this sun sign commit themselves to public service by running for positions of power. In fact, power and authority are what these opportunists are ultimately after. That's what they've built their life around.

Capricorn Success Potential Profile

This is the original success story, the legendary self-made man—the individual who builds his own business from scratch on his own from the ground up. He poured the cement and he put on the roof. Nobody else did.

Fiercely ambitious, he embodies the spirit of capitalism, and worldly successes—power, wealth, and recognition—are almost always his for the struggle. (If he survives or undertakes the struggle.) In fact, he is one of the most commercially ambitious signs in the zodiac and is the most success-oriented.

This is not a showman. This is a serious, professional businessman, who simply works his way up the ladder step by step—cautiously, patiently, enduring hardships, and responding to challenges all along the way. A social climber as well, he courts the wealthy, the cultured, and those in power. Eventually he wins, but at his studied pace it takes him longer to do it.

Capricorns who are successful have undertaken a substantial struggle. They eventually grab the power they set out to acquire years ago. Now, on their own, they are secure at the top—wealthy, proud, dignified, respectful of tradition and authority, and surrounded by tasteful furnishing, important friends, and a loyal family. They made it. They usually do. All it took was total commitment.

ZODIAC MANAGER'S CAPRICORN STRATEGY

- Have no doubts: This is a professional. Whatever the task, few will do it better and in a more businesslike manner. Capricorn will expect you to be businesslike as well, and the more he respects your professionalism, the greater his loyalty. If you run a loosely organized business, Capricorn will not be interested unless you are asking him to organize it.

- Keeping Capricorn involves career planning. Capricorn wants to know what he needs to get to the top and what he needs to do each step of the way to get there. He will want to know what the rewards are at each step as well. Capricorns are addicted to master plans, so if you want him to stay around, make certain he understands what plans and rewards you have for him.

- Perks are powerful. Anything you can do to add a sense of dignity and prestige to Capricorn's life—do it. A country club, the right social organization, dinners at the best restaurants, an impressive company car/parking place, introducing him to the local influential—these feed Capricorn's insatiable appetite for social status, whatever his actual position in the company. The higher up the ladder, the more exclusive the perks. And don't forget to include frequent praise in the perk category.

- Frequently, Capricorns are not the most popular employees on the payroll. Be prepared to smooth some ruffled feathers of those who have felt snubbed, put down, sharply criticized, or avoided. Capricorn often has a single-track mind and, when focused, he is blind to the sensitivities of others around him. Capricorn's arrogance, even in the early stages of his career, will be particularly difficult for your seasoned veterans to take, so pointing out Capricorn's productivity and performance record can ease some tensions. In addition, let Capricorn work for one of those who have been bruised and he will make them look good through his efforts. Whenever in a meeting, make sure there is a moderator who can temper Capricorn's remarks or put them in a less abrasive perspective. Capricorn is too valuable to dismiss so whatever can be done to turn down the heat is very much worth doing.

- Punctuate Capricorn's life with fun. Lurking underneath this serious, success-driven, workaholic is a cynically humorous individual. Relieve the pressure he puts on himself with "time outs." Capricorn needs the break from himself, and so do you and your people.

- Stress stability and security. Capricorn needs to operate and command from a comfortable, protected nest within a comfortable, protected environment. The past is as important as the future, and it assures Capricorn that he has a solid foundation on which he can do his work and build a career. A changeable and fragile organization is not for him. Capricorn is not an office temp. He wants to be around for the long haul.

- Keep all lines of communication wide open. You will want to know what Capricorn is doing at all times because what he is doing is invariably important. Track his performance, because it is most certainly having an effect on company performance. He is so tied to your and the company's success that he becomes the vital link in explaining why things are working as well as they are. Knowing his dissatisfaction or inability to get the results he wants is just as important. You may need to remove some obstacles along the way that are dampening productivity (and guaranteed, Capricorn can tell you who or what they are).

- Force people on him. Capricorn is so confident, so controlled, and so self-contained that he will avoid most people at work and do the job all by himself because, after all, he can do it best. That's what he believes. And he's wrong. Force him to meet the other talented people in the organization. Force him to open up and discuss issues without prejudice. Get him to listen to other viewpoints and, above all, experienced voices. Capricorn believes he can learn from doing. He also needs to learn from others and to work with others. One of the toughest jobs you will have as a manager is getting Capricorn to respect people enough to work side by side with colleagues and not look down on them or discount their contribution. A "people person" Capricorn, though rare, is pure power and performance.

- Raise Capricorn's success quotient to the highest power by becoming "friends." For all his outward stoic strength, he desperately needs TLC—but TLC of the "respected boss" variety only. Whoever is in charge of seeing that Capricorn's career goals are met should also strive to be one of his most supportive friends. This will not only help Capricorn achieve the stable life he so very much desires and build in his loyalties, but, even more important, it goes a long way towards humanizing Capricorn, enhancing his value to the firm and life. A fully realized, mature, well-rounded Capricorn is possibly the most dominant personality in the zodiac, but to realize it, his personal life must be given as much of a chance to be a complete success as his professional life. A few great friends as well as a great family will help achieve it.

Capricorn Most Profitable Positions		
Accountant	Historian	Physician
Administrator	Hospital Administrator	Plumber
Air Traffic Controller	Hotel/Motel Manager	Police Officer
Architect	Insurance Agent	Politician
Banker	Internal Revenue	Producer
Chemist	Service Employee	Purchasing Agent
Chief Executive Officer	Investment Manager	Real Estate Broker
City Manager	Judge	Researcher
Civil Servant	Lawyer	School Administrator
Computer Programmer	Life Scientist	Self-Employed
Construction Industry	Lobbyist	Soldier
Employee	Machinist	Sports Official
Controller	Manager (Planning,	Statistician/
Critic	Organization)	Mathematician
Diplomat	Management	Stock Broker
Draftsman	Consultant	Systems Analyst
Economist	Manufacturer	Teacher
Editor	Museum Curator	Technician
Engineer	Musician	Underwriter
Entrepreneur	Office Business	Wholesaler
Farmer	Manager	
Geologist	Pharmacist	
Head Hunter	Physicist	

Capricorn Most Profitable Location

Any place in America—big city, small town, and farmland—you can find a profitable Capricorn office. It's the office of the boss. The old-fashioned capitalist is definitely in charge, and his office reinforces that. It has a conservative, impressive dignity about it with traditional splendor and great taste in furniture, flowers, and artwork. It is also a place where a great deal of serious, patient work is done. This is a useful office occupied by a clearly important businessman.

However, since Capricorn spends so much time here it also has the feel of home or a comfortable den. Its trappings reflect stability, security, and the privacy Capricorn needs to protect himself from those insignificant others.

Capricorn Job Skills Rating			
1 (Poor) to 5 (Excellent)			
Communications	4	Interpersonal Skills, Teamwork	3
Learning and Thinking Skills	4	Punctuality, Efficiency	4
Work Attitude	5	Loyalty	5
Creativity	3	Technology Skills	3
Problem-Solving	4	Self-Confidence	5
Decision-Making	4	Enthusiasm, Motivation	3
Money Management	5	Self-Management, Initiative	5
Flexibility	3	Honesty, Integrity	5
Accountability, Responsibility	5	Visionary	3
Planning Skills	5	Leadership	5
Details	4		

MANAGING CAPRICORN RELATIONSHIPS

In General

Capricorn pursues relationships as cautiously as he does everything else in life. After all, this is a reserved, undemonstrative, and rather formal individual who has totally committed himself to his career, and only people who can help him get where he is going are of any value to him. To others, he can be condescending and careless of their feelings.

In his professional life Capricorn chooses friends who are like himself: conservative, intelligent, hardworking, productive, and dedicated. He will also surround himself with socially and financially prominent people who convey a sense of security to him that he has made it among the very best. Capricorn is an opportunist, and his relationships reflect that. Although his relationships are reasoned, logical, and usually unemotional, Capricorn does need recognition and praise from him friends/workers; in fact, although he won't acknowledge it, he can use a lot of emotional stroking to keep him healthy and secure.

In his personal life he is a devoted family man, projecting a kindly, yet disciplinary, father image. Although he can be tough, he is firm and just, with a strong sense of responsibility for those in his care/employ. Critical, demanding, and at times cold, he nevertheless is a very reliable, kind, faithful friend to those few he has selected to be around him. But more often than not, Capricorn can be found alone, struggling to make his way or in his executive suite at the top.

Summary

Capricorn Working Relationships		
PROFITABLE	RISKY	NON-PROFITABLE
Virgo	Taurus	Aries
Capricorn	Gemini	Scorpio
Pisces	Cancer	
	Leo	
	Libra	
	Sagittarius	
	Aquarius	

Bottom Line

Capricorn with Capricorn

This is a powerhouse of a pair, and if one doesn't try to take control from the other you can expect very profitable results. Clearly a partnership with equal and separate responsibilities is called for here. It would be hard to find a smarter, more hard working team; there is no duo more dedicated to making the painstaking climb to the top. Doubly conservative and careful, yet doubly profit-oriented, you can expect major results from this superior match.

Capricorn with Aquarius

Capricorn is a street-smart, hardworking capitalist who can see the advantage of employing this curious, intelligent, scientific explorer. But conservative Capricorn must also be smart enough not to restrict the independent Aquarius to the point that he cannot innovate and experiment if he is to make this a big money duo. Aquarius has trouble working for anyone but himself, and, because he is a high-powered, energetic performer and a risk-taker, he could drive Capricorn crazy. But Capricorn knows the value of money and he will try to put up with this rebel in exchange for profit—at least temporarily.

Capricorn with Pisces

The street-smart, practical Capricorn manager needs Pisces's creative intelligence. Pisces needs an enlightened boss who can compassionately guide him towards productivity, and Capricorn is the one who fits the bill. Capricorn is a caring moneyman who is careful not to upset Pisces's fragile emotional nature. Granted, Capricorn's disciplined work style is in total contrast with Pisces's unstructured dreamlike style, but as long as Pisces is productive, Capricorn will be most tolerant. Remember, though, Capricorn is a dyed-in-the-wool capitalist and Pisces has got to fulfill his end of the commercial bargain as he goes.

Capricorn with Aries

These are two very dissimilar personalities, and it is difficult to imagine this duo working together for very long. The faster-moving Aries has no time for Capricorn's more cautious style, and because each is a take-charge personality, they are bound to clash when it comes time to make decisions.

Aries's unstructured, frantic, commercial life and high-risk spending and experimentation don't fit in at all with this financial conservative, who slowly grinds out results only after serious deliberation. There's nothing to recommend pairing these two.

Capricorn with Taurus

These two are very similar personalities: hardworking, conservative, committed, persistent, and capitalist. Slowly but steadily they force their way to the top. This is a powerful and successful duo, which, unfortunately, will find great difficulty in working together. Both Taurus and Capricorn want to be number one and in total control. However, because there is big-league profit-making potential here, it is hoped that a partnership could be arranged with equal responsibilities on both sides. These are two very strong personalities and the balance would always be delicate, but the high-powered results are worth the risk. You'll know soon enough if it's going to work out.

Capricorn with Gemini

There are two very smart, coolly calculating sun signs here. They will get along very well on a mental level. However, it will not be easy keeping them together unless the conservative, one-step-at-a-time Capricorn is willing to allow Gemini to continue to work in his fast-paced, future-oriented, multidirectional world without restraint. There are big profits to be made here, so it is certainly worth the effort to pair them. Capricorn needs Gemini's exploration and inquiry, and Gemini could use Capricorn's solid business skills to pull all the activities together into a profitable package. If each can be tolerant of their personal differences, impressive results will follow.

Capricorn with Cancer

In many ways, these two signs are at odds. The more creative, aggressive Cancer will have difficulty understanding the serious, committed, capitalist Capricorn, yet Capricorn needs a creative complement to his personality, and Cancer is a good choice. Capricorn is usually mature enough to provide for the care and feeding of Cancer in such a way as to help him become more efficient and productive. Cancer needs help to become commercial, and, as long as what he offers can turn a profit, wise Capricorn management can help him realize that. You won't find a Cancer boss strong enough for Capricorn, but as long as Capricorn doesn't try to overpower Cancer or make harsh demands, this could be a money duo.

Capricorn with Leo

Conservative Capricorn could certainly use the public relations and promotional skills of the dynamic Leo. This is an area that the reserved, dignified Capricorn is weakest in. However, Capricorn doesn't respect Leo's flash. Capricorn is serious about his traditionalist reputation and his classy, tasteful style and demeanor. As far as he is concerned, Leo is a clown. But Leo is a smart clown, and his antics bring in business. Capricorn is aware of this, too, and, as much as he doesn't want it, he will need Leo as a front man. There will always be friction and blow-ups between the two, but they can be profitable together if they don't have to cross paths too many times.

Capricorn with Virgo

There isn't anything the responsible, industrious, dedicated Virgo assistant wouldn't do for a boss he respects and admires, and Capricorn is a boss who fits that bill. In this pairing, Capricorn has all the help he needs from an aide who is just as committed to the enterprise as he is. These are two very similar personalities except for one very fortunate difference: Capricorn wants to lead, and Virgo wants to serve. Capricorn will be well served by this tough administrator, who will see to it that Capricorn's orders are obeyed. Sometimes Virgo may come on too strong, even to his Capricorn employer, but that is the small price you pay for having a perfectionist who makes it all work so smoothly.

Capricorn with Libra

Capricorn managerial skills can make Libra's entrance into the pressure-filled, commercial world possible if Libra is productive. Libra is a breed apart from the capitalist, career-oriented, profit-making Capricorn. However, his analytical skills can be profitable to the always learning Capricorn. If Capricorn can temper his demanding, do-it-my-way nature (and he will do almost anything to make money) and carefully manage Libra's skills in a protective way, this can be a productive pairing. However, it is not a natural relationship, but one based solely on a Capricorn need, and if Libra doesn't produce it will be all over (except for Libra's bruises, which last a long time).

Capricorn with Scorpio

These two sun signs are rivals. Each is after control and power. Both are calculating and manipulative.

Capricorn with Sagittarius

If only they could get together. The adventurous, far-flung Sagittarius makes things happen in a dozen different ways. Capricorn can take all those things, put them together, and make them profitable. Sagittarius explores and creates; Capricorn plans and manages. This could mean big money. The problem is that the battle will be between Sagittarius's freedom and Capricorn's control. However, the capitalistic Capricorn will probably be smart enough to realize that because Sagittarius's freedom brings in the dollars, enlightened management is called for. As long as Capricorn can appear to keep his hands off, and as long as the money comes in, the opportunistic Capricorn will hang on to this delicate relationship.

ASTRAL FAX #10: "GOING HOME"

The day-to-day demands on professional businessmen are more intense than ever. What kind of real-life partner can give you the kind of personal lifestyle you want, free from the pressure of the work place? What kind of person do you want to go home to? Here is who you will find astrologically when you open the door. Then you decide which one is for you.

Aries: If you have a fast-paced job, you can anticipate little relief at home. Aries's energy and enthusiasm will keep you just as busy and active as your job. Also you can count on loyalty from your mate, and in exchange you will be expected to honor the demands of this at-home boss. This is "life" in the fast lane.

Taurus: The all American, apple-pie and baseball home life awaits you. Expect high values and principles with intense loyalty. You enter a well-ordered home with a mate expecting your total love and affection as well as some gifts now and then. Taurus will also be strong and independent when it comes to their personal activities and will want your support. Prepare to give 100 percent to this mate.

Gemini:　Chances are you will find a slightly different personality each day you go home—on the days your mate is actually at home, that is. Never boring, this multipersonality sun sign is always on the move. This mate has a strong need for self-expression, and many signs find it difficult to stay with such an independent spirit. However, if you provide the security you will have a front-row seat at a fascinating circus.

Cancer:　This is a real family sign expecting total devotion in return for loyalty. This is a true domestic mate, hosting a comfortable home that is secure and warm. Expect Cancer to want children and a household full of friends and family on the holidays. Only highly principled and honorable signs need apply for this mate.

Leo:　Go home to find warmth, devotion, love, and support from a Leo mate. But your mate will also want to be treated as a very special person. Leos need to be prominent, so the "house" must show your mate off and you will need to support his strength to your colleagues and friends. Leo will entertain lavishly and frequently, while also having time for children whom he adores.

Virgo:　Virgo takes relationships very seriously. Total commitment is important, and in exchange you can expect total loyalty and devotion. Because a long-term relationship is what this sign wants, Virgo will go to extremes to discuss every detail and make certain the relationship is always on solid ground. Expect all the values of honesty and thoughtfulness here from a very practical partner in search of the special romance.

Libra:　Relationships are vital to Libra to relieve the loneliness they frequently feel in their soul. As a result this mate will work hard to make your life together comfortable and meaningful. Expect a real partnership here, working together to make a loving life together. Libra goes out of his way to make your coming home—and life at home—a warm experience.

Scorpio: Open the door to a dominating personality who is in charge of this relationship. This partner is also very loyal and most desirous of helping you achieve. Competitive by nature, Scorpio will spend at-home hours advising you on how to succeed. For the aggressive, goal-oriented sun sign, this is an excellent coach to have on the sidelines.

Sagittarius: Charm, fun, and enthusiasm are what you find when you go home to Sagittarius. You will also find, however, a free spirit who does not like to be controlled and who speaks his mind freely and openly. Home will be a spontaneous and exciting place, but don't expect games to be played when it comes to feelings and emotions. For the strong at heart and gainfully honest—only.

Capricorn: Security and stability are important to this mate. Marriage is forever, and love is the source of his strength. Also expect a dominance from the sign in an ever-present attempt to keep the relationship strong. More than any other sign, love is the goal with Capricorn, and, if you play by the rules, he will always be waiting for you.

Aquarius: Not always home when you arrive, this freedom loving sign is frequently off pursuing his interests. The Aquarian world is much bigger than the home and he doesn't compromise. This is not someone to lean on, or to expect to be there for you, but in return, you get an exciting, ambitious, independent individual to watch and admire while you get on with your life.

Pisces: For those sun signs who want someone to be totally dependent on them and who want loyalty and devotion in return, Pisces is the one to go to. Pisces wants a person to support them and take over the controls of their life. In return, you get warm love and the joy of experiencing one of the more creative spirits of the zodiac. At this house, you're the boss.

XI

Managing Aquarius

January 21–February 19
Symbol: Water Bearer
Ruling Planet: Uranus
Element: Air
Motto: "Do Your Own Thing"

A HISTORIC SAMPLING OF THE AQUARIUS WORKFORCE

Hank Aaron	Susan B. Anthony
Mikhail Barishnikov	Judith Blume
Humphrey Bogart	Garth Brooks
Helen Gurley Brown	Thomas Edison
Clark Gable	Wayne Gretzky
Carole King	Mary Leakey
Charles Lindbergh	Douglas MacArthur
Toni Morrison	Paul Newman
Jack Nicklaus	Yoko Ono
Franklin D. Roosevelt	Gertrude Stein
Margaret Truman	Lana Turner
Laura Wilder	Oprah Winfrey

A Confidential Listing of Your
Aquarius
Managers, Employees, and Colleagues

Name	Birth Date	Position

INTRODUCING AQUARIUS

An Air sign, Aquarius is ruled by Uranus, the ancient Greek name for Heaven, or night sky. This vast, open sky symbolizes this sign's openness to far reaching new ideas, knowledge, and ways of thought. Aquarius lives in a world of advanced thought, which shapes her unique personality. Frequently eccentric and certainly independent, Aquarius thrives on going it alone.

Curiously, for a sign that prefers detachment, Aquarius is also noted for humanitarian acts. And although she is drawn to helping causes, she isn't easily drawn to close personal relationships.

Aquarian intelligence, principles, imagination, foresight, and intuition make her one of the more interesting and complex signs in the zodiac. Careful handling is required to transform her into a commercial quantity, but Aquarian uniqueness makes it worth the effort.

Aquarius Energy Profile

Get ready for continuous energy, spontaneously spent. This is a nervous, restless, impulsive sun sign that is always active, always coming from and going to, something in an emergency or changing direction. So much is going on in the life of an Aquarius that she dares not sit still. In fact, sitting still is an activity she loathes.

Everything about Aquarius is motion, making her difficult to keep up with. Hyperactivity in several directions at once from this human generator makes it hard for anyone to stay close to her or work with her. Always busy, always frenzied and frantic, Aquarius runs about, overflowing with projects and trying to accomplish a million different tasks, satisfying her unending curiosity and experimentation, and fulfilling her obligations to help others. Fast-paced is the way she prefers it even though many find it disrupting and occasionally irresponsible. Aquarius can't, and won't, stop moving. There's too much to be done.

Aquarius Personality Profile

Be prepared for the unexpected. Eccentric, unpredictable, erratic, rebellious, and difficult to know, this revolutionary may be the most original and complex personality in the zodiac. Cool and detached, we are still attracted to her attractive magnetic personality. This highly changeable and spontaneous individualist is a unique, one-of-a-kind specimen, who seems to be creating her life as she lives it. Never a dull moment, this personality is always surprising us with her exciting and diverse pursuits. She is always flying high, and usually flying alone, which is the way she prefers it.

This is above all the sign of freedom and liberty. In fact, nothing is more important to Aquarius than to be able to do whatever she wants to do with no restrictions or limitations. She must roam free and will not be caged by anybody. Aquarius will do nothing that will compromise her freedom, and, as a result, she is able to march to her own drummer, living life her way. This commitment to freedom extends to others as well. "You live life your way, I'll live life mine." Live and let live. This means Aquarius lives life as she wants, not as it is, frequently creating an unrealistic world around her.

Aquarius is progressive with both eyes on the future. In fact, her mind spends most of its time in the future. She is a genuine visionary and trend setter whose forward-looking insights spot the new ideas well in advance. What she can see now is usually the wave of the future, even though it sounds far out.

A noted humanitarian and social reformer, Aquarius is out to create a world of peace, love, and brotherhood. With a kind of blind idealism she seeks to find utopia, where we can all lead the best possible lives.

Because of her intense independence and her innovative mindset, Aquarius has an unusual, eccentric lifestyle. She's fascinated by the out of the ordinary and the bizarre and on the lookout for out of the way places, people, events, and alternative lifestyles. She has a smorgasbord of things she wants to do, and life is her playground to explore. Life to her is Disneyland, the zoo, the aquarium, the planetarium, the museum—any place she can investigate and analyze something new. Aquarius is basically a discoverer, versatile and adaptable to any brave new world—which makes her also interested in and adept at the occult sciences.

Aquarius is an idealist with a strong ethical and moral code of conduct. She is trustworthy, honest, and fair, and she expects others to be as well. Those who aren't and those who are hypocrites are written off immediately. Outwardly, she is friendly and caring, but because of a strong self will and a free spirit, she can be narcissistic and independent. This aloofness (bordering on being cold) has become a real Aquarian trademark. She is attracting and attractive but at the same time cool and detached (like royalty).

Emotionally detached, Aquarius suppresses feelings and funnels her ideas. This tends to prevent Aquarius from becoming close to others and from developing any meaningful ties to people or community.

Distant and enigmatic, Aquarius is also unpredictable. You never know what's going on for sure, and you're always too far away to understand. Once committed to an individual, Aquarius is faithful and loving, but it doesn't mean she is totally accessible. This makes her the zodiac's most intriguing, yet maddening, personality. No question, you won't fully understand Aquarius nor get very close to her, but you will find it exciting (and possibly even frustrating or confusing) to be around her.

Aquarius Intelligence Profile

The mature Aquarius could be labeled brilliant, brainy, even genius. The most curious sign in the zodiac, Aquarius is a born student. She loves to think and she thinks quickly. She is extremely interested in, and very serious about learning. In fact, this sun sign is more brain than body, more mental than emotional.

The kind of learning Aquarius is interested in comes from experience, not school. Self-taught, Aquarius learns from everything she does and from everywhere she goes. She is an investigator with a high degree of curiosity, perception, insight, and psychic ability. She is an analytical thinker with great intuition and foresight, and it will be her mind that will lead us into the next decade. Aquarius has the ability to comprehend the future, now. She will lead us to the forefront of scientific technology or new philosophical theories with her active, foreward-looking mind.

With worldwide interests, this lively mind is constantly seeking stimulation. She is known for her brainstorming, innovative, and brilliant ideas coming from out of the blue. She is an independent thinker and cares nothing for popular opinion. It's her thought that counts. She is also trusting only to her opinion and is not tolerant of the thoughts of others; in fact, she could care less what others think.

Another warning: Once Aquarius has reached a conclusion or finds a solution, her mind closes like a steel trap. Once she believes she knows the answer, a rigid mind takes the place of an open one, and she is done searching.

Finally, because she is so quick to decide, her rational intellectual process sometimes breaks down, and her confusing lifestyle occasionally causes her to forget what she has learned, but overall Aquarius is operating with an overwhelmingly inquisitive, impressive brain.

Aquarius Communications Profile

Her genuine humanitarian instincts make her a sympathetic and caring conversationalist. Sincere and kind, she is willing to help you work out any problem. Although Aquarius rarely shows her own feelings or emotions, she is concerned about you and will use her considerable knowledge and insights to ease the pain or help you in a course of action.

Aquarius is an interesting communicator, preferring to interact one-on-one, or in small groups, on issues of importance. But expect what she is talking about to jump all over the place. Little will logically follow what went before it and the whole experience can seem off the wall. Aquarius knows what she's talking about or she doesn't talk at all, so be prepared to debate anything you say to her that is weighty. This is a hard-nosed inquisitor who won't let a thought-provoking comment slide by without being discussed.

You will also notice that Aquarius is a good listener. But if you are espousing views that are contrary or of little interest to her, she doesn't care what's being said; she is simply being polite.

Aquarius Diplomacy Profile

Because of her involvement in social and philanthropic causes, Aquarius is forced to exhibit occasional diplomacy, and her honest sincerity and genuine concern make her very good at it. However, outside those affairs that are precious to her, don't expect Aquarius to be anyone other than her own person, with her own mind.

In every other situation, Aquarius is too self-possessed and too independent to play diplomatic games. She knows she's right, and she isn't afraid to make that clear. Aquarius believes she is simply being honest; others may consider her tactless. Other factors working against Aquarius are her intellectual seriousness and her tendency to debate every issue—characteristics not always welcomed at polite functions. Aquarius is simply too much of a restless rebel and too eccentric to fit in with folks who are just trying to be civil for a few casual hours.

Aquarius Money Profile

She's erratic. Aquarius doesn't really understand the value of money, nor is it a major concern in her life. As long as Aquarius has all the freedom she needs, she really doesn't care about money.

Yet Aquarius can be seen handing her dollars over to the needy. She can also be a sucker for get-rich-quick schemes, fast-talking salesmen, and slick advertising. Aquarius can be a speculator and a risk-taker with a mixed record of success. She can just as easily preach, "Don't go into debt" and "Don't run up charge accounts!" Aquarius needs a money manager, although chances are she won't listen to her. As usual, she thinks she knows best, but where money is concerned she's wrong about that.

Aquarius Loyalty Profile

To those in true need (and who are basically worthy individuals), all you have to do is call Aquarius. She will come to your aid intellectually and financially, although not emotionally. Aquarius is devoted to helping. Aquarius is also faithful and loyal to her very closest friends and to her family. You don't always notice it because of the famous Aquarius aloofness and independence, but she is loyal to the tight circle around her (as long as they don't feel trapped by it).

Winning Aquarius's loyalty is almost impossible. You truly have to be a productive, ethical, and valuable citizen, or she has no time for you at all. Winning her loyalty is like climbing Everest, and it probably won't last forever—but it is a rare victory worth cherishing.

Aquarius Work Habits Profile

To some extent it depends on how interested she is in the job itself—Aquarius is easily bored with routine and any nine-to-five job—but if the job is exciting, challenging, and explores the unknown, you'll have a very satisfied, hardworking employee. In the right job, Aquarius will be at it 24 hours a day. Aquarius is a very intelligent worker with superb analytical powers. Her research skills are unrivaled, and you are bound to profit from her uncanny ability to see into the future and to describe tomorrow's market today. This is an experimenter and innovator who, through trial and error, is trying to make sense out of the future.

However, Aquarius is interested in so many fields that her efforts can quickly become disorganized and she can become irresponsible. Totally involved with so many things at once, Aquarius may become ineffective, overall, unless she is carefully managed. But—and this is most important—only enlightened and subtle management works for Aquarius. Because she considers herself so independent and is so smart (and always right), she does not take orders easily. In fact, in her view she knows much more than the boss will ever know—she is also more perceptive and more intuitive. Not only does this freedom-loving employee resent authority, but she resents having to be caged inside an office, she resents having to be on time, she resents regulations, she resents detail, she resents having to go to meetings, and she resents having to keep to a schedule. In short, she resents having to work for someone else. And that's what you have to overcome when you hire an Aquarius employee, not to mention the fact that she will never make a decision.

On the surface, Aquarius appears to like all levels of people, but she prefers to work alone on her solitary mental investigations, scientifically, philosophically, or creatively exploring original ideas. She is a researcher who needs the freedom to explore and experiment. Every job must be more fascinating than the last, or you will lose her and her energy. Highly structured, conservative, production-line companies can forget about Aquarius. She is too spontaneous, eccentric, and unpredictable for their corporate culture to encompass. Furthermore, Aquarius can only be productive if her brain is constantly feeding and dreaming in an open environment and if her curiosity has the freedom to pursue new dimensions and new directions.

An appropriate profession involving social causes attracts the humanitarian aspect of Aquarius. This side of Aquarius is perfectly capable and very willing to help those in need and those she considers deserving. This philanthropic Aquarius is more focused and more conservative than the exploring Aquarius. But because both these sides exist in every Aquarius, she may switch from one aspect to the other over the space of one hour.

Impatient and living to do everything in the now, this sun sign loves change and travel. She is also more of a thinker than doer, and, when she becomes bored, her energy level stalls at zero and she becomes commercially useless.

Difficult to manage, Aquarius is out for herself and her ingenious futuristic ideas. It is the challenge of the job, that attracts her, not the company or the people. She will work only by her rules, which don't always make any business sense to anyone else, but if you can accommodate her unconventional attitude and her independence her dreams could mean big money.

Aquarius Leadership Profile

This is not a leader. This is not a boss. Aquarius isn't interested. Aquarius is an investigator, not a decision-maker. She could care less about giving orders or representing an entire corporation. To her leadership is intellectually dull.

In fact, Aquarius executives are endangered species or rare collectors' items. But if you ever do find an Aquarius boss, expect her to be the hands-off variety. She will allow great freedom for her workers, and as long as they produce they have a job. She will expect her workers to work independently, just as she does, but seriously, and she won't care how they get the answers just as long as they do.

Aquarius Success Potential Profile

Aquarius can be very successful at discovery and developing new ideas and technology. She can be successful as a philanthropist helping her fellow man. Successful as a freelancer, an entrepreneur, an inventor, in a job where you work close. But her path through commercial life is not a conventional one. Not ambitious in the accepted capitalistic sense of the word, this independent rebel is looking for untried avenues, for constant challenges and for just plain excitement in life. She has no passion for business, although her adventuresome spirit can lead her into the unknown, and her discoveries can be commercially valuable, even though that wasn't the intent of the journey.

Aquarius tends to be at odds with the existing world order because she doesn't really live in it. She isn't interested in the present, but rather in the future. She is interested in the unexpected and the new. She will appear to be not of this world—unreliable and unprofitable. But Aquarius doesn't care what anyone thinks. She doesn't need anyone's help. Aroused by curiosity and humanity, Aquarius explores the playgrounds of life seeking new ways and new ideas. Operating outside the mainstream of society, her measurement of success is judged on her own purely personal terms.

ZODIAC MANAGER'S AQUARIUS STRATEGY

- If the job requires creativity, innovative thinking, futuristic design, research, and analysis, and if it can be performed in a structureless, freewheeling environment, then you've found your employee in Aquarius. (Do-gooder vocations included.) Few signs require as specific a job description as Aquarius, but then, Aquarians march to their own drummer. You are simply borrowing them for a while until they go off into another universe of excitement.

- Aquarius can be of value to a more traditional firm if her eccentric individualism can be trimmed a bit and replaced by some pragmatism. That is the only way for her to add real value to most businesses. Her unrealistic disregard of time, schedules, structure, and accountability can cause serious disruption, and she must be made to understand the consequences of her independence. Everyone else suffers. This lesson in business must be made clear to Aquarius. Compromise, on everybody's part, is necessary for success.

- With any Aquarian you will be forced to face the issue of separation is integration. Independent Aquarius will fight integration, and you can't afford separation. Negotiation will be continuous. Tradeoffs on each side must be made. Prepare to support times when Aquarius can do it on her own in exchange for times when she becomes a team player.

- Frequently invite Aquarius to sit down for an informal chat. Find out what's on her mind. You won't be disappointed. Aquarius is always thinking and exploring, and much of what she is creating doesn't relate to the work she's doing for you. However, it could be valuable, so don't let anything drop between the cracks. Remember: She's the most curious sign in the zodiac, and the ideas she comes up with may mean profit to you.

- An overmanaged Aquarius is an unhappy, unproductive worker. Hands-off rather than hands-on management is what she is hoping for. Few commercial enterprises can go that far, but be prepared to give her as much space as you can. Consider, for example, using her only as a freelancer or an outsource, or let her telecommute. Keep the organization structure away from her as much as possible. When Aquarius feels free, she does her very best work. So "Free Willy!"

- Don't expect to make a best friend. Aquarius's impersonal nature doesn't allow for closeness. Her heart is off limits to you as well as to her. You are employing a mind, not a body and soul. You are wasting your time if you think relationship management will improve her performance. Her brain is what you are paying for, and it's all you are going to get.

- Offer Aquarius perks such as retreats, think tanks, and seminars—any place where she can launch her loftiest ideas and test them out with other brains. Let her grow on your time, and she is more likely to produce on your time.

- Your organization and your executives must hold high principles and values. Honesty, integrity, and respect are very important to Aquarius and they must be important to you. Aquarians will not work in a dishonest or sleazy business.

- Support a cause. Aquarian interest in humanitarian efforts, social progress, or philanthropic organizations is very strong, and your interest will be noted and recorded. Aquarius's respect for you (and perhaps a bit of loyalty) can result.

- Solitude is important to her work. Don't feel you should be constantly surrounding Aquarius with people for fear she will be lonely. At peak productive times she wants to be lonely. Remember that she doesn't need anyone else to get the job done. She is all she needs.

- Accept her eccentricity and, in appearance, clothes, and work habits, her originality will shine through. If you strip her of her badge, you prevent the "real" her from coming through the door. Her highly personalized demeanor is a statement of her free-spirited independence and a conservative, corporate dress code will only serve to make her feel like one of the masses instead of one of a kind.

- Yesterday's Aquarius is not today's. This is an ever-changing individual whose unpredictable actions will be a constant surprise. Expect surprises and be prepared to address them one at a time. For example, in the morning you may think you have won her over to your way of doing things only to find out in the afternoon she's working for the rival across the street. You must be continuously alert (behind the scenes) to make sure you have the freshest, current insight on Aquarius and her intentions. No obvious spying is allowed, so this is not an easy task. But then, Aquarius is very frank about what's happening, so just ask.

- With rapidly changing conditions, every company needs a futurist. For best results, handle with care and Aquarius can launch you into the world of tomorrow today.

Aquarius Most Profitable Positions		
Actor	Geologist	Psychiatrist
Architect	Hospital Administrator	Research and
Astrologist	Inventor	Development
Astronomer	Lobbyist	Employee
Author (science fiction)	Marketing Researcher	School Guidance
Chemist	Meteorologist	Counselor
CIA Official	New Product Developer	Scientist
Computer Programmer	Nurse	Self-Employed
Creative Idea Man	Occupational Therapist	Sociologist
Criminologist	Oceanographer	Social Worker
Economist	Operations Research	Space Program
Engineer	Analyst	Employee
Entrepreneur	Philanthropist	Statistician/
Explorer	Physical Therapist	Mathematician
FBI Agent	Physician	Systems Analyst
Freelance	Physicist	Technician
Futurist	Politician	Travel Agent
		Veterinarian

Aquarius Most Profitable Location

This is a highly animated, curious, and independent individual. Whatever she is interested in, she pursues it on her own terms. The job is no more important to Aquarius than the location. She goes anywhere to do what she wants. This is a highly versatile explorer who is just at home in New York City as she is on a farm in Nebraska. As long as she is feeding her mind and has the freedom to follow her own path, she is able to perform.

But if she does need a home base to work in, it must be a large, modern, open–space filled space, with every high-tech, futuristic marvel on the market. Aquarius needs to work in an environment that touches the future.

Aquarius Job Skills Rating			
1 (Poor) to 5 (Excellent)			
Communications	3	Interpersonal Skills, Teamwork	3
Learning and Thinking Skills	5	Punctuality, Efficiency	3
Work Attitude	4	Loyalty	3
Creativity	5	Technology Skills	3
Problem-Solving	4	Self-Confidence	3
Decision-Making	3	Enthusiasm, Motivation	4
Money Management	3	Self-Management, Initiative	5
Flexibility	3	Honesty, Integrity	4
Accountability, Responsibility	4	Visionary	5
Planning Skills	3	Leadership	3
Details	3		

MANAGING AQUARIUS RELATIONSHIPS

In General

Fiercely independent, Aquarius feels trapped by close relationships. People from all walks of life are drawn to the apparently friendly Aquarius, but they are usually kept at arm's length. Aquarius's eccentric lifestyle and frantic energy level simply precludes lasting friendships, and that is fine with Aquarius.

Aquarius prefers to be impersonal. She wants people to love her ideals and her efforts, but not her. Purposefully blind to the feelings of others and lacking compassion, Aquarius gets in exchange the freedom she needs to live life her way. Friendly with many and close to very few, Aquarians are frequently on the lookout for new faces, which forces a frequent turnover among Aquarian acquaintances. Of course, that's fine with Aquarius, who prefers quantity to quality, as well as forgetting the past and moving on to the much more interesting future.

This sun sign does get great pleasure out of humanitarian relationships, but all friendships are less important than her personal and professional freedom. Her detached coolness serves as a barrier to understanding. This isn't a follower, and her solitary attitude makes her difficult to work with. Once she commits herself, she can be temporarily faithful, but the fact remains that many more people try to know Aquarius than she tries to know them.

Aquarius is an excellent judge of human nature, but she will always remain a puzzle to herself and others. It's ironic, even with her reserved nature, her independence and enigmatic personality, people are still drawn to, and really do like, Aquarius.

Summary

Aquarius Working Relationships		
PROFITABLE	RISKY	NON-PROFITABLE
	Leo	Aries
	Virgo	Taurus
	Sagittarius	Gemini
	Capricorn	Cancer
		Libra
		Scorpio
		Aquarius
		Pisces

Bottom Line

Aquarius with Aquarius

The frantic, independent activity of these two makes it impossible for them to work together. These are two entrepreneurs, not coworkers. They have great respect and affection for one another, and each loves to know what the other is working on, but they don't want to do it together. No profit is to be gained from pairing these two freedom-loving spirits. In fact, by doing so you restrict their individual experimentation and their productive capabilities.

Aquarius with Pisces

These sun signs have several things in common: philanthropy, a psychic sense of the future, and novel ideas. But the similarity stops there. Aquarius is a doer and finds little in common with the dreamlike world of Pisces. Energetic Aquarius hits out in many different directions; Pisces dwells quietly in one. And Aquarius is so very independent that she isn't about to stop for a fragile, sensitive Pisces—no matter how creative she is. Aquarius is simply too self-centered to include Pisces in on her fast-paced, multidirectional game. Besides, they have something else in common: Neither has particularly strong business skills.

Aquarius with Aries

These two will meet occasionally and share fascinating stories, but soon each is off again on her own very personal adventure. If you can capture those occasional moments, you will be treated to some terrific ideas/stories/ experiences, but don't expect that meeting to last very long. Both Aries and Aquarius know what they want and are strong enough to go after it on their own. And they are much more valuable and happier working independently than together.

Aquarius with Taurus

The moment the Aquarius employee walks into the Taurus office she will feel trapped. Taurus knows only one way to work: by the strictest, capitalist manifesto you can find. The freedom-oriented Aquarius would be totally shut down; her skills are unable to operate in such a closed environment. Taurus could certainly use the brilliant, forward-looking, inquiring Aquarius mind, but because she adheres to her conservative rules, Taurus would soon restrict Aquarius from operating independently, which is the only way Aquarius can be productive.

Aquarius with Gemini

These two have a great deal in common. They're two restless, investigative minds with a whole world to explore. The experiences these two bring back are exciting. Their perceptions and insights can be brilliant. But work together? Why should they? Nothing really to be gained from it other than sharing fascinating wisdom. But these two are so independent and so detached from the commercial world that they can't sit around telling stories. They need to be off, alone, living them.

Aquarius with Cancer

Aquarius is simply too powerful and independent to hang around with the emotional and cautious Cancer. In fact, the pairing could hurt Cancer. Aquarius grants philanthropic gifts or a helping hand to such people as Cancer, but she would never accept her as an equal. Cancer simply is not up to the world-class performing speed of Aquarius, nor is she self-assured enough to contribute to the Aquarius's book of knowledge.

Aquarius with Leo

This is an exciting and potentially profitable duo. However, Leo will have to get off her throne and forget about pushing this employee around. This is by no means a natural relationship, but if Leo will give up her passion to control and allow Aquarius the freedom to do it her way, there is big money to be had here. Leo will simply have to become a mature, understanding, and responsible manager, as well as hold back the criticism she is bound to have for the more frantic, unconventional Aquarius worker. They're two very different performers, but if Aquarius does bring home the dollars, Leo will do about anything to make the pairing work.

Aquarius with Virgo

The strict, disciplinarian Virgo employee could certainly make organizational sense out of the frantic, uncoordinated efforts of her Aquarius boss. In fact, Virgo's administrative skills are exactly what is needed here if Aquarius is to become efficient and profitable. But will Aquarius allow herself to be watched over this closely? Virgo is a tough perfectionist, and this will never be to Aquarius's liking. But it is a productive pairing if Aquarius is willing to give up some of her freedom for a more effective enterprise.

Aquarius with Libra

Libra searches for balance and harmony. Aquarius pursues the future. These are opposites! Aquarius investigates, uncovers, changes, rearranges, and explores, as Libra is trying to piece together the puzzle, putting it into a peaceful existence. This may be the original odd couple. In fact, Libra could suffer emotional bruises in this pairing. Aquarius is simply too frenetic and too revolutionary for the emotionally struggling Libra, who wants to be left alone in a calm and protected room.

Aquarius with Scorpio

There is nothing the Scorpio boss would love more than to tame her Aquarius employee and control her otherwise frantic exploration. Aquarius, of course, refuses any trap restricting her freedom and is strong and sure enough of herself to fight off the possessive Scorpio and keep her freedom. Scorpio would never have the satisfaction of owning Aquarius, and that's part of her reason for existing: controlling everyone and everything around her. Aquarius is wise enough to keep her independence and avoid slavery.

Aquarius with Sagittarius

These are very similar, freedom-loving, and investigative personalities. But their love for freedom and their independent self-confidence will make it very difficult for them to work together. They certainly will enjoy sharing experiences and ideas, but working together day to day can stifle their experimentation. This can be a highly profitable duo if they are only loosely associated and come together only on selected occasions to present the results of their latest adventures. It won't be easy to keep them in a room long enough to make it all productive.

Aquarius with Capricorn

Capricorn is a street-smart, hardworking capitalist who can see the advantage of employing this curious, intelligent, and scientific explorer. But conservative Capricorn must also be smart enough not to restrict the independent Aquarius to the point that she cannot innovate and experiment if she is to make this a big-money duo. Aquarius has trouble working for anyone but herself, and because she is a high-powered, energetic performer and risk-taker, she could drive Capricorn crazy. But Capricorn knows the value of money, and she will try to put up with this rebel in exchange for profit—at least temporarily.

Astral Fax #11: "Turning the Tables" or "Exposing the Boss"

What the stars reveal about employees, they also reveal about the boss.

Richard Jenrette, retired chairman of the Equitable Companies and co-founder of the investment banking and securities firm Donaldson, Lufkin, and Jenrette, astrologically analyzes his management qualities and weaknesses as well as those of other signs, in his book *The Contrarian Manager.*

Want to know all about an Aries boss from an Aries boss? Read on:

"An Aries like me must be the boss (or think we are)...You can't be the boss. We start our own company. Also, rams are stubborn—we fight fiercely and stubbornly when adversity comes. We're also very truthful, sometimes too truthful for our own good. But I also learned the Aries native has several key weaknesses and knowing them helps me mitigate the effect. For example, Aries are notorious for starting too many things and not finishing them. Knowing this, I try (not always successfully) to avoid starting too many things and I make sure I finish them. Thinking about what the other person is like, capable of and thinking, helps me be a better manager. Astrology has also helped me understand myself better. Astrology helps me (and can help you) understand and appreciate the differences in how each of us responds to events."

XII

Managing Pisces

February 20–March 20
Symbol: The Fish
Ruling Planet: Neptune
Element: Water
Motto: "To be or not to be: That is the question"

A HISTORIC SAMPLING OF THE PISCES WORKFORCE

Ansel Adams	Ruth Bader Ginsburg
Alexander Graham Bell	Erma Bombeck
Elizabeth Barrett Browning	Johnny Cash
Glenn Close	Julius Erving
Jackie Gleason	Mikhail Gorbachev
George Harrison	Patty Hearst
Michelangelo	Liza Minelli
Anais Nin	Linus Pauling
Knute Rockne	Dr. Seuss
Elizabeth Taylor	Ivana Trump
Harriet Tubman	Gloria Vanderbilt
George Washington	Joanne Woodward

A Confidential Listing of Your Pisces
Managers, Employees, and Colleagues

Name	Birth Date	Position

INTRODUCING PISCES

A Water sign, Pisces is ruled by Neptune, in mythology, the god of the deep, dark ocean. With its symbol, the Fish, think of Pisces as swimming in the ocean of life. Their choices are to swim peacefully along, daydreaming in calm waters or swimming deep below the surface into the darkest parts of the sea.

The few Pisces who choose the more adventurous course often achieve enormous success. The others survive as sensitive, compassionate, and creative spirits. Because of this duality it is difficult to profile a "typical" Pisces.

Pisces can be ultra-sensitive and easily bruised. They can also be dreamers and have a sense of unreality about them. They can be interested in too many things. They can seek escape from the harsh world. The question becomes: "How real-world mature is the Pisces who you are dealing with?" For Pisces also appears in the ranks of America's wealthiest more than any other sign. You just have to "fish" for the right one.

(Note: Rarely do you find a typical Pisces. There is a chameleon quality to this sign that makes him harder to pin down than the others. Some of the following characteristics may appear contradictory. However, that is simply reflective of the complexity of this sign.)

Pisces Energy Profile

More the bystander than a player, this is a passive sun sign with a low energy level. Very little incites the disinterested and removed Pisces into action. The majority of the time, Pisces can be found dreaming, preferring his fantasy world of illusion to the world of reality. He can also be lazy or take the path of least resistance. You see, Pisces is the fish swimming against the current: Every inch is a monumental struggle. So rather than struggle upstream, most Pisces settle back into a calm, quiet, unhurried environment and daydream about the future, rather than do anything about it.

However, you will meet an occasional Pisces who has made the arduous trip upstream, and this is the energized Pisces who will really go places against all odds. This is a Pisces who will make the strenuous effort to get ahead. But keep in mind this is the rare Pisces. Most Pisces simply refuse to overcome all worldly barriers, preferring instead the safe, calm, peaceful waters of home.

Pisces Personality Profile

Pisces's basic weakness is his inability to understand or want to understand who he is, his true self. So enamored with magickal worlds and imaginary fantasies, he is always avoiding himself and how he fits into the real world. As a result, he fails to grasp the essential factor that could help him grow and achieve. He fails to realize he has a choice in life as to how he wants to live and what he can accomplish: He can swim all the way to the top or he can remain a bottom feeder. Most Pisces fail to understand that they have a choice in life and retreat, preferring instead a superficial involvement with reality, shielding themselves from the world.

This tendency to escape can also involve some troubling health problems. Pisces seem to have a high incidence of alcohol and drug addictions as they try to erect walls around their imaginary world.

However, because Pisces has a charming, laid back, good-natured manner, few people sense the turmoil inside him.

Another important characteristic of Pisces is his emotional make-up. Pisces is the lover of the zodiac. He craves the romantic (people and places), and the warm glow hovering around a Pisces in love is a remarkable light. This is an affectionate, compassionate, loving individual who is immensely super-sensitive. Sympathetic, trusting, or kind—you name the emotion, and he is guided by it. Naturally, because he so easily exposes his soul and feelings, he is totally vulnerable, even to the passing stranger, and it is easy for anyone to take advantage of this giving and gullible sun sign. Because he cares so much about what others think of him and he needs to be needed, he is easily hurt and often withdraws into a protective shell. (Although some will use laughter to hide their injury or insecurity.) As a result, Pisces is always on the edge of becoming a real loner who feels no one understands him, cares for him, or appreciates his talents. Easily troubled and easily discouraged, this is not a self-confident sun sign.

On top of all this, Pisces seem to be cursed with genuine hardship. It is indeed a struggle for him to overcome life's barriers to happiness and to a peaceful romantic existence. Even if by chance Pisces has a vision in his mind of what he wants, he rarely is able to turn that vision into reality. As a result, most Pisces remain big dreamers, not doers, and live in a make-believe world of unattainable fantasy. He simply never overcomes the odds against him and retreats into a comfortable, easy life of pipe dreams. In the extreme case, he stops caring about tomorrow and only cares about his plight and the unfairness of life. (And his life does seem unfair.) He becomes an escapist and people write him off as a cranky oddball, weak, lazy, and a careless hermit who's detached and indifferent.

Fortunately, there is a plus to be found: Pisces is creative—very creative, and that is the gift he has been given to survive with in this difficult and competitive world. But, unfortunately, another negative isn't far behind: Pisces is not especially fit for such a competitive world. Granted his is artistic and imaginative, but he doesn't know how to make himself commercial, nor does he have the strength to climb over all those roadblocks to become successful. The world could really use his creativity and sincere compassion, but it's unlikely many will experience it. For Pisces, success may come about on a minor level, working in a comfortable environment and with the support of very close friends. In safe circumstances, Pisces can transform his visions into reality and provide a small band of followers with delightfully personal music, poetry, film, etc. And on this small scale you can sometimes witness a charming, loving Pisces, exploring his vivid imagination, free from the pain of reality.

Another plus is that Pisces is the original healer and caregiver. Filled with compassion and sympathy, he gives over much of his life to helping and nurturing others (ironically overlooking himself in the process).

At the core, Pisces's lack of self-confidence is most crippling. He has even convinced himself that he won't make it. He constantly underestimates his fighting spirit and his talents. But with encouragement (he is very susceptible to others' opinions) and strong support, the very best of the Pisces can enter the ring and emerge a winner. In fact, those top Pisces who do go to war and who are tenacious enough to stay the course can come out very big winners. And when he has overcome as many barriers as Pisces must, the sky is the limit—as long as he can encase his emotions in steel against the outside world.

Pisces Intelligence Profile

This is a highly magickal and independent, creative mind. Artistically gifted, Pisces possesses a vivid and unique imagination. He also possesses superb intuition, which easily makes up for any lack of scholarship. Don't get me wrong, Pisces is a very capable learner and can recall facts easily, but he tends to rely more on his cunning perception and insight. The fact is that Pisces prefers to go off on his own and "feel" his way through a problem. Don't expect to find a logical, disciplined, and decisive mind here, although Pisces believes he is being perfectly logical. Quick and clever,

Pisces is creatively intelligent in his own very special way, and don't under-estimate his smarts because he doesn't "think" as you do. Also, don't be surprised by his extraordinary psychic ability to see exactly what is soon to happen.

Pisces Communications Profile

Much of the time, Pisces is detached and shy, but he is also a bit of an actor and frequently calls on his acting talents to protect him against emo-tional broadsides and to hide his real feelings. Pisces uses conversation as knights used their shields. Humor, stories, charm, compliments—anything to keep you from getting at him. A cruel word from someone can do grave damage here, and Pisces will babble on about nothing to stave off such a wound. This naturally results in confusing statements and vague sentiments, which leave a listener confused. Of course, that's the way Pisces wants it. But as a consequence, very few people are able to get through this verbal barrier, and this isolates Pisces even more. A casual discussion with a Pisces reveals almost nothing about him. He will talk to you all day but reveal little of himself. And beware: He will also prefer the dramatic story to the truth just to keep the conversation flowing.

On the other hand, if you are in need, Pisces becomes the most sympa-thetic, caring listener in the zodiac. In fact, he will listen forever if you let him, and, in the process of that listening, he will encourage and inspire those who are suffering to overcome their problem and fight their way back to good health. Honestly compassionate, he is the one the lonely should turn to.

Pisces Diplomacy Profile

On the surface, although shy, Pisces can be charming and fun. And because many diplomatic settings are polite and civil, this sun sign could be comfortable. His concern for others and his genuine interest in people are big advantages here as well. However, the creative side of Pisces may not find anything to be offered at such an affair, and there is always the danger that his sensitivity may be bruised or his integrity and compassion ques-tioned. However, he could probably survive the diplomatic circuit. But the question is: Does he want to?

Pisces Money Profile

Most Pisces are not money-makers. Most have to come to grips with too many barriers before they can turn a dollar. But regardless of whether they can make it or not (and they worry about that all the time), brother can they spend it—freely!

Pisces's emotions rule his finances, and only a very stern money manager can save Pisces from living on the edge of bankruptcy. For Pisces, money buys comfort, dreams, toys, and pleasure—everything he needs to help him escape. The joys and fantasy that his money can buy relieve his struggle in life. And if you're a good friend, an employee, or someone in need, Pisces will be very generous.

But back to "how does he earn it?" True, most Pisces do not make much money, but they do marry or inherit it. And then there is Lady Luck! Pisces can make it big on the craziest promotion, wheeler-dealer, get-rich-quick schemes ever dreamed up. Naturally, the dollars never stick around very long, but who can blame him—he gets so much fun out of spending them. And he will enjoy it just as much if you spend your money on him.

Pisces Loyalty Profile

Loyalty is extremely high on the Pisces's list of life's priorities. And he is dying to be faithful and dedicated to anyone and anything—that is, if they are as kind, supportive, and encouraging to him as he is to them. Pure kindness is really all Pisces ever asks for. This is one of the few true loyalists on the Earth. But be forewarned: He wounds easily, and the moment he feels you have been unfaithful, his dedication will switch to "off" immediately, and it is virtually impossible to turn it on again. Because Pisces's loyalty is virtually religious in nature, you assume a substantial responsibility to Pisces in return for his loyalty. And this loyalty can extend not only to an individual, but also to the corporation, belief, or country. Indeed, Pisces can be the dedicated "true believer," if what or who he believes in has never caused him pain.

Pisces Work Habits Profile

Pisces is creative—even though it is hard for him to market that skill. He can be trusted with large-scale responsibilities—providing the pressure is off. He is extremely perceptive and can spot things others overlook. His intuition and psychic skills will show you the future now.

No doubt about it, the world could use his creative intelligence and foresight (not to mention his compassion for his fellow worker), but we don't often get to see those Pisces's qualities in the market place.

Pisces frequently miss the commercial boat. He simply has a tough time making money off of his talents. To begin with, he is primitive when it comes to selling—himself or anything else. He lacks the discipline and the routine needed to perform a nine-to-five job. He dislikes confinement and is slow and reluctant to reach solutions and make decisions. He lacks the concentration and the intensity to finish a job. Easily bored, he loves the big pictures but not the details. And the bottom line: He is not competitive. Pisces has an impractical, fantasylike, otherworld view, which does not fit in the capitalist style. And rather than giving business advice, he should be seeking it.

If Pisces is to become a valuable performer, he will need help in developing his self-confidence and efficient and productive work habits. But there are other problems. His changing moods and his escapism are difficult to deal with.

His career is an issue he probably hasn't thought much about. Pisces doesn't seem to be in control of his life. He seems to float about. He seems lost in the commercial fish tank, and it will take sympathetic and caring guidance from enlightened management to help this employee succeed and become profitable. One way is to constantly monitor and applaud his work. Another way is to put him on a team of talented, creative, cooperative, and understanding co-workers. And by all means, give him a quiet open space to work in that is comfortable, attractive, and surrounded by positive people.

Of course, there is that rare Pisces we've talked about (the one who does swim upstream) who can sell himself. This is that individual who decided from the start that he would climb every obstacle and jump every hurdle. He has escaped the Pisces dream world and dived headfirst into the real world. Reality has made him strong and self-assured. This rare, motivated Pisces is a star worker and a one-of-a-kind employee that you will never want to replace. He has all the Pisces skills—perception, creativity, foresight, and the big picture concern for humanity—but the difference is, he knows how to turn those skills into money for himself and for the business.

Pisces Leadership Profile

It is difficult to imagine most Pisces as leaders. His lack of goals, discipline, and indecision alone should eliminate him—not to mention his personal preference for working behind the scenes instead of in front. He could, of course, decide to be his own boss (with extreme and varying degrees of success, as he pursues the "big dream"), but to command others is virtually impossible. Pisces's self-confidence (when it exists) usually comes not from within, but from those around him. A true leader must have the inner strength to know he is headed in the right direction.

Pisces has no desire to command or dominate and finds it very difficult to make the commercial commitment to climb the corporate ladder. He generally feels unqualified for higher positions of responsibility. Pisces's confusing attitudes toward life and his lack of career planning are additional stumbling blocks. Pisces prefers to serve rather than rule, and that seems to be a wise decision.

Pisces Success Potential Profile

In general, the Pisces view of the world is not corporate-oriented, nor is competitive capitalism of interest to him. Most Pisces have little worldly ambition and little interest in power, rank, or wealth. Greed, both private and professional, plays no role in his life. In fact, very little the world has to offer ever exists for Pisces, with the exception of those who are suffering and in need of his compassion, care, and charity.

And there is, of course, the other Pisces: the Pisces who is willing to swim upstream, accept the challenges, struggle, and make his unique mark in the commercial world. But for the most part, Pisces takes the easier route downstream. He will procrastinate or decide "life's too difficult." He'll accept his fate and exist outside the competitive world. This unmotivated and vulnerable Pisces could eventually become a societal misfit, marching to a different drummer, as the real world passes him by at a great distance.

True, those Pisces who go for the gold can end up being some of the strongest most successful individuals in the zodiac, but, more likely, the trip is too bruising for this easily wounded sun sign and life becomes for them a small, but calm, private pond.

ZODIAC MANAGER'S PISCES STRATEGY

- Clearly the less structured, less formal, and less traditional your organization is, the easier it will be for Pisces to fit in. However, the more difficult it will be to make Pisces productive. The truth is, a total free-wheeling environment is not what freewheeling Pisces needs if he is to produce. He needs to understand exactly what role he must play to contribute to your success. He needs some rules and guidance in order to come down to Earth and get real. Otherwise you'll get ideas, tons of incredible ideas, and mystical, magical, inventions—but not necessarily the ones you need and are paying for.

- Attention to the hiring process is paramount. You must go as far as you can to uncover Pisces's real career intentions and how strong they actually are. You might be completely candid about your job description so Pisces knows exactly what he's getting into, what his responsibilities are, and what your expectations are. Because Pisces seem to quit their jobs more frequently than any other sign, a sound and thorough interview is critical. Avoid surprises by both parties with an open, candid, and lengthy hiring session.

- It is vitally important for Pisces to feel an emotional connection with his job and company. What he is offered must be the kind of work he can lose himself in and become totally devoted to. To perform well, Pisces must not feel detached or disenfranchised. Not only must the job and the company "want" him and be emotionally satisfying, but those around him must also want him to be a valuable part of their effort. The more Pisces is needed and the more his feelings can relate to what he is doing, the more committed, productive, and loyal he will be.

- Although Pisces will delight in working with employees who are as creative, innovative, and intuitive as he is, a strong Earth sign supervisor (such as Taurus, Capricorn, or Virgo) can help him perform even better in the commercial sense. These are the types of partners who can keep him on schedule, on time, and on course. A sensitive, practical manager is necessary to keep Pisces's efforts in touch with real business demands. Find a real-world partner who can guide Pisces's performance, and you will be on your way toward getting full value out of this miracle-working, imaginative sun sign.

- Keep in mind Pisces's desire to be of service to others. Place him in a position where he can help new people in the organization and share his experience with them. Give him an opportunity to work with any charitable causes you support. This sign is born to nurture others, and the more you can feed this inner need, the happier, more productive, and more loyal he will be.

- Respect Pisces's original mind. There will be times when his fantastical mind will take off and soar in unknown directions. Let him go. Who knows what incredible ideas he might come back with. And when his mind does return to Earth, make sure you are waiting there to download his mystical adventure.

- Work with, not against, Pisces's independence. This may be the worker you hire as a freelancer, outsource work to, or allow to telecommute. A flexible, more creative job arrangement may be the clue to making Pisces a commercial success.

- Be sensitive to certain personal problems Pisces might have as a result of his escapist nature. Be prepared to discuss tardiness and no-shows—not to mention substance-abuse problems. Careful, however, that you don't accuse him wrongly. If you do, and you're wrong—he's gone.

- Remember that you're working with a most independent, imaginative, and supernatural mind. The match between him and capitalism will never be perfect, so know when you've gone as far as you can go to get him into the company mold. And beware also not to destroy his remarkableness in the process. His value is in his uniqueness and although some conformity is necessary to get jobs done, too much conformity can wipe out his best quality: creativity.

- Be prepared, also, for the capitalistic Pisces, the one who is swimming upstream to success and glory. His talent still is his amazing imagination, but to this you add his ability to direct it toward a commercial goal. If you are lucky to catch this Pisces, put him in charge of other creative sun signs in your organization. The power Pisces understands them, the creative process, and how to make it all come together in the real world. This is an invaluable executive, and the profit-making interpreter and director of all your creative types.

Pisces Most Profitable Positions		
Actor	Home Economist	Philosopher
Artist	Horticulturalist	Physical Therapist
Author	Hospital Staff Member	Plant Nursery
Cartoonist	Hypnotist	Manager
Chef	Industrial Designer	Poet
Clergyman	Interior Designer	Psychic
Commercial Artist	Inventor	Psychoanalyst
Creative Idea Man	Magician	Railroader
Dancer	Merchandiser	School Guidance
Dietician	Musician	Counselor
Employment Counselor	Nurse	Sculptor
Entertainer	Occupational Therapist	Singer
Explorer	Oceanographer	Social Worker
Fashion Designer	Philanthropist	Travel Businessperson
Graphic Designer	Photographer	Veterinarian

Pisces Most Profitable Location

His requirements must be met for him to work at all. Pisces's needs include an open workspace in the midst of his own creative colleagues, a free space conducive to sharing ideas and supporting one another's efforts. Management can watch from a distance, but the harsher business end of the commercial enterprises can disrupt this productive creative venture if it intrudes. Pisces and his coworkers must be able to feel that they are free to persue their ideas without restraint. An open and supportive atmosphere is the only one in which Pisces can be productive. And this environment should be as romantic as he is, with striking views, luscious colors, dramatic lighting, mood music, and comfortable furniture—a real pleasure palace, for that is where Pisces feels most secure.

Pisces Job Skills Rating			
1 (Poor) to 5 (Excellent)			
Communications	5	Interpersonal Skills, Teamwork	5
Learning and Thinking Skills	3	Punctuality, Efficiency	3
Work Attitude	3	Loyalty	5
Creativity	5	Technology Skills	3
Problem-Solving	4	Self-Confidence	3
Decision-Making	3	Enthusiasm, Motivation	4
Money Management	2	Self-Management, Initiative	4
Flexibility	4	Honesty, Integrity	5
Accountability, Responsibility	3	Visionary	4
Planning Skills	3	Leadership	3
Details	3		

MANAGING PISCES WORKING RELATIONSHIPS

In General

Of course the relationship Pisces prefers most is one of true love. Romance is critical to his happiness, but because he frequently picks the wrong partners, his moods are of the roller coaster variety.

When he is healthy (physically and mentally), Pisces can be the great American neighbor. A real pal and everybody's friend, his first instinct is to help. However, although Pisces is very eager to aid others and to please, he desperately needs to be appreciated in return. For Pisces, devoted companionship and sympathetic friendship is essential, and he will go to extremes to get them. Friends can make or break Pisces. If they aren't around to support him, watch out for major escape from reality and a retreat with a hermitlike existence.

Don't expect to understand Pisces very well, but don't be afraid to tell him all about you. He cares and he listens, but he is so vulnerable that he can't afford to reveal much of himself for fear that he will be hurt. This is an impressionable individual whose strength and confidence depend on how those around him treat him. He needs your encouragement and support. If he has it, he will return the favor many times over. To Pisces, happiness and love are friendship.

Summary

Pisces Working Relationships		
PROFITABLE	RISKY	NON-PROFITABLE
Leo Capricorn	Taurus Cancer Virgo Pisces	Aries Gemini Libra Scorpio Sagittarius Aquarius

Bottom Line

Pisces with Pisces

These two highly imaginative dreamers operating in their own factory world that is undisciplined, unstructured, and distinctly uncommercial will enjoy one another's encouraging and supportive company. Very little that is profitable will come out of such a pairing. However, slip in a gentle, sympathetic manager who is results-oriented and you have a chance to make some big dollars off these two creative idea-makers. Don't cut off their freedom to operate, but they will need caring, capitalistic guidance if they are to produce.

Pisces with Aries

There's very little here to recommend the commercial pairing of these two. The brash, energetic, creative, and self-confident Aries will find nothing special about Pisces and certainly won't take the time to discover Pisces's creative skills. Pisces, on the other hand, needs support and encouragement from a partner, and Aries is not that kind of sun sign. Aries can easily hurt Pisces, and it's best these two stay apart in the harsh commercial world.

Pisces with Taurus

The cautious, conservative Taurus boss has a great need for the futuristic, imaginative mind of the Pisces employee, and the Pisces employee will find Taurus to be a compassionate, caring, and patient boss. However, Taurus is bedrock capitalist and, if after all this careful nurturing of the creative, undisciplined Pisces, he doesn't produce, Pisces will be out—and fast. The test is whether Pisces can work under an eventual deadline and can accept the fact that he must be commercially profitable for his commercial, yet sympathetic boss.

Pisces with Gemini

The self-assured, multidirectional, energetic Gemini is the kind of cool, calculating individual who can do damage to the emotionally fragile Pisces. There is nothing profitable about this duo. Pisces wouldn't be given a moment of Gemini's time and certainly none of the tender loving care that the creative Pisces needs to exist in the real world. The coolly intelligent Gemini has no interest in the day dreaming Pisces, commercially speaking.

Pisces with Cancer

Pisces and Cancer will be shy at first, then attracted to one another. These are two very compatible, creative spirits who work on a sensitive and emotional wavelength. They will understand and support each other. However, alone they are not disciplined enough to be productive. If their creative ideas are to provide profit, a gentle, sympathetic manager is absolutely necessary to keep them on the commercial track. These two are capable of wonderfully imaginative ideas, but whether they are money-makers depends on a compassionate boss.

Pisces with Leo

Who would suspect the strong, fierce, dramatic Lion could seek a vulnerable, sensitive Pisces employee? The key is Pisces's highly creative and farsighted mind. This is exactly the kind of new world employee that Leo loves to have on him stage. Pisces can create the kind of theatricality Leo thrives on, and Leo, under the surface, is the kind of encouraging, compassionate, and sympathetic boss that Pisces must have. As long as Leo allows Pisces the freedom to operate, this could be a highly profitable venture-capital type of duo. Big risks are taken here, but big money is possible in return.

Pisces with Virgo

The demanding Virgo and the undisciplined Pisces are two opposite personalities. Yet, if Pisces is to be profitable, he needs this kind of partner. Virgo has the business skills to turn the highly imaginative Pisces into an efficient, productive money-maker. But the price the freedom-loving, sensitive Pisces pays may be too high. Virgo may hold the reins too tight and require too much of the unstructured, freewheeling Pisces. And Virgo's critical nature can be damaging to the emotionally vulnerable Pisces. Still, if Pisces can adjust, and if Virgo can be flexible, there is a chance for money here.

Pisces with Libra

Indecisive Libra and indecisive Pisces are handily a productive duo. These two aren't really born for a commercial world and, in fact, have constructed worlds of their own away from that harsh competitive arena. Their business skills just aren't strong enough to give them an advantage whether alone or together. They are emotionally and personally compatible, but they just aren't disciplined enough to be profitable.

Pisces with Scorpio

The sensitive, emotionally vulnerable Pisces would be wise to stay clear of this demanding, possessive Scorpio boss. Scorpio will see profit potential in creative Pisces, but Pisces should see only trouble. Pisces needs a sympathetic, caring boss—not the driven, egocentric dynamo. Scorpio will never understand the freedom or the unstructured environment Pisces needs if he is to become productive. For Scorpio, everyone does it his way or not at all. Pisces should stay away from this duo if he wants to avoid serious emotional injury.

Pisces with Sagittarius

Here are two friendly, creative characters who will enjoy one another's stories and company. However, there is very little to be gained from a commercial company. Sagittarius prefers his independence and his multidirectional lifestyle. He isn't interested in being the enlightened manager to a sensitive, imaginative, and vulnerable dreamer. Sagittarius is a non-stop doer, and he simply doesn't have time to slow down for the fragile Pisces.

Pisces with Capricorn

The street-smart, practical Capricorn manager needs Pisces's creative intelligence, and he is willing to make concessions to get him. Pisces needs an enlightened boss who can compassionately guide him towards productivity, and Capricorn is the one who fits the bill. Capricorn is a caring moneyman who is careful not to upset Pisces's fragile, emotional nature. Granted, Capricorn's disciplined work style is in total contrast with Pisces's unstructured dreamlike style—but as long as Pisces is productive, Capricorn will be most tolerant. Remember—Capricorn is a true capitalist, and Pisces has got to fulfill his end of the commercial bargain as he goes.

Pisces with Aquarius

These sun signs have several things in common: philanthropy, a psychic sense of the future, and novel ideas. But the similarity stops there. Aquarius is a doer and finds little in common with the dreamlike world of Pisces. Energetic Aquarius hits out in many different directions; Pisces dwells quietly in one. And Aquarius is so very independent that he isn't about to stop for a fragile, sensitive Pisces—no matter how creative he is. Aquarius is simply too self-centered to include Pisces in on his fast paced, multidirectional game. Besides, they have something else in common: Neither has particularly strong business skills.

ASTRAL FAX #12:
FIRING POINTS, THE FINAL CHAPTER

Firing an employee is never easy and never fun. But how you do it often helps the employee accept the verdict more easily. Your firing points should avoid the sun sign's known strengths and focus on their known weaknesses.

Aries: Avoid firing based on a lack of creativity and cutting-edge achievement. Focus on a lack of attention to productivity and detail.

Taurus: Avoid firing based on a lack of productivity, performance, and loyalty. Focus on lack of people skills and compassion.

Gemini: Avoid firing based on preventing individual initiative, energy, and new business ventures. Focus on the failure to focus and continuous growth.

Cancer: Avoid firing based on a lack of commitment, people skills, and compassion. Focus on inadequate leadership and results.

Leo: Avoid firing based on a lack of leadership, charisma, and public relations value. Focus on a lack of consistent improvement and lack of detail.

Virgo: Avoid firing based on a lack of productivity, results, and commitment. Focus on a failure to delegate and play with the team.

Libra: Avoid firing based on a lack of judgment and fairness. Focus on a lack of growth, direction, and decision-making.

Scorpio: Avoid firing based on a lack of direction and perseverance. Focus on the inability to delegate and allow for independent decision-making.

Sagittarius: Avoid firing based on a lack of building new business, creativity, and courage. Focus on failure to commit to corporate goals.

Capricorn: Avoid firing based on a lack of leadership and financial results. Focus on a lack of delegating and team-building.

Aquarius: Avoid firing based on a lack of adventurous new ideas and independence. Focus on failure to fit in and commit to the corporate mission.

Pisces: Avoid firing based on a lack of creativity and sensitivity toward people. Focus on inadequate strength and direction to build sales.

Index

Author Bio

Joe Taylor Ford created and wrote "Astral Answers," an astrological advice column that appeared in *The Boston Herald, The Chicago Sun Times,* and for papers in Orange County, California. He also wrote feature articles such as "An Astral Analysis of The Boston Red Sox" and an "Astral Analysis of The Boston Mayoral Race."

Mr. Ford is currently president of Words, Ink, an international communications consultancy. Words, Ink publishes more than 50 different titles in the communications field and has a database of 20,000 buyers.

Mr. Ford is also publisher of *The Executive Speechwriter Newsletter,* a bimonthly newsletter of quotes, jokes, stories, and ideas for the executive speechmaker. Clients/subscribers have included the White House Communications, Interior Secretary Bruce Babbitt, Denny Crum (head basketball coach, Univ. of Louisville), Lou Holtz (former head football coach, Notre Dame), Richard Marriott (vice chairman, Marriott Hotels), Jack Welch (chairman, GE), D. Wayne Calloway (CEO, Pepsico), William Howell (chairman, J.C. Penney), Blaine Hess (president, Thomas J. Lipton), Senator Robert Dole, Ron Barbaro (president, Prudential Insurance), Jack Laughery (chairman, Hardee's), Bud Hadfield (founder, Kwik Kopy), and Pat Williams (general manager, Orlando Magic), among others.

Mr. Ford is the author of the musical *The Last Minstrel Show* starring Della Reese and Gregory Hines, which was produced at the Dupont Playhouse in Wilmington, Delaware, and the Locust Theatre in Philadelphia, Pennsylvania.

A graduate of the International School, Mr. Ford has a B.A. in Classics from the College of the University of Chicago and an MBA in marketing from the University of Chicago Graduate School of Business. Mr. Ford is former assistant dean of the School of Business, University of Connecticut.